MOM

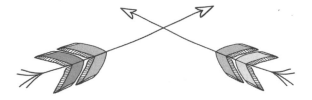

Learning to Embrace
What Matters Most

AMY RIENOW

Published by Randall House Publications
114 Bush Road
Nashville, TN 37217

Printed in the United States of America

13-ISBN 9781614841036

For my Beautiful Mom—
who inspired me to desire motherhood
as my first and most satisfying career.

For Alice—
to show how valuable you are.

Table of Contents

Acknowledgements

To my husband and best friend Rob—not many men would have the faith and courage to have seven children, which alone is a great adventure, but also step out in faith to live this life of ministry. As in the words of the Greatest Showman, I do love "walking the tightrope with you" and I always know that you will be there to catch me when I fall! Thank you for loving this whole family with all your heart. I love you!

To RW, Lissy, JD, Laynie, Milly, Ray and Rush—being your mom makes me feel so privileged because I am daily thankful and truly amazed that God chose ME to be your mom. Each time I welcomed one of you into our family it felt like I won the lottery! Life is so RICH because of all the LOVE each of you bring to my heart.

To my Mom—thank you for giving me my first vision of the joy of motherhood and for creating so much happiness in our home that the whole family still wants to come to Grandma's house and Bop-Bop's pool! Thank you Dad for loving Mom so well and being a spiritual leader to this large family.

To Andi—I did not think it was possible to edit as quickly and efficiently as you did for me during this process. I would not have made my first deadline without your help. Thank you!

To Kari—I cannot tell you how much I appreciate all that you and Jonathan have done and are doing for VFM, but most of all, thank you for your friendship.

To Meg—we entered motherhood about the same time, and many of the lessons in this book come from countless conversations at McDonald's® playlands. I am so thankful that we have been able to cry together about our kids' struggles and also celebrate ALL their successes. I continue to learn so much from you!

To Michelle Orr and the Randall House team—thank you for giving me the idea and the opportunity to write this book. Without your prodding, I am not sure if and when I would have taken on this project!

Most of all, thank you Jesus! You are my best friend and my first husband. May I love You more day by day. I am so grateful that You never, ever give up on me!

Introduction

The words centered at the top of the Greenhouse school newsletter are still fresh in my mind. Greenhouse is where my kids attend their school co-op once a week. Tom Spacek—headmaster—usually writes a few words of encouragement to inspire parents as we endeavor to educate our children. I often skip reading the short paragraphs because I am kind of a lazy reader—preferring to find out what I absolutely need to know. This time was different.

A paraphrase of a quote by G.K. Chesterton jumped off the page and hit me squarely between the eyes: "Whatever is worth doing, is worth doing poorly."[1] *Really?*

While I cannot remember for sure, I was probably in the middle of another day where I felt I was "doing poorly" in many areas of responsibility. Or better stated, I was "doing poorly" at simply being a mom.

I should be a mom who keeps the house clean and organized. I should be a mom who takes my kids to the library on a weekly basis with a well thought-out list of all the good books I want them to read. I should be a mom who is much more physically fit and gets up early to exercise. I should be a mom who cooks healthy, frugal meals for her family. I should be a mom who is gentler and less harsh with her words. The "should be" list was endless.

Of course, that was my list for me. There were many other lists. A list for each child and a large list for my husband. They should be lots of things, too!

The kids should be well behaved. The kids should love to read. The kids should have good friends. They should be smart and should not watch too much TV, or maybe no TV? The kids should be good at sports if they enjoy sports. The kids should not be forced to play sports if they do not enjoy sports. The kids should memorize more Scripture. They should be perfect. Sounds ridiculous, right?

If you had told me in my high school, college, or even during the "married before kids" years that I was a perfectionist, I would have laughed in your face. Me, a perfectionist? Me, the girl who figures out how many classes she can skip and still get an A or B. The girl who is always late unless there is some major consequence for being late. The girl who can't seem to keep her space organized or clean. There is no way this girl is a perfectionist. I am not even a Type A personality. At least that was what I thought!

Yet, thanks to Tom Spacek, G.K. Chesterton, and the Flylady (more about her later), I was learning something very important about myself. Being a perfectionist had little to do with having perfection in any area of my life. Instead, it was all about *desiring* perfection.

Truth be known, I did not see any perfection in my life: not in me, not in my husband, not in my kids, and not in my circumstances. But I secretly wanted it! It was a sometimes spoken but more-often unspoken drive. These unrealistic subconscious desires were affecting me daily because I felt I was missing the mark.

I regularly lived with discontent, feelings of failure, a heaping amount of guilt, and an unnecessary lack of joy and gratitude. I say it was unnecessary because I had every reason to be filled with joy! However, because I was convinced I should be doing a much better job at being the mom I wanted to be, I too often sacrificed that joy.

The learning did not stop there. I realized this perfectionistic drive was having a negative effect on the relationships I was desperately trying to build and nurture. Thankfully, I was beginning to learn while my kids were all very young that perfectionism destroys relationships, especially between mother and child.

Relationships are what life is all about. I will not bore you with a list of countless movies that relate the story of a successful person with all the wealth and power one could ever want, but who instead has an empty life because he has no relationships—no love, no connections, no family.

I knew I wanted my kids to have healthy relationships—overflowing and abundant. I knew that my kids would be the most successful if they were relationally successful, and that relational success started in the home. Primarily, it started with me.

While this book is about my transformation as a mom of seven children and what I have learned through this journey, I am writing to encourage every mom.

I've been married to my wonderful husband, Rob, for 24 years. However, I will not mention him much in this book. There are two reasons for this decision.

The first is that I had to come to a point in my parenting where I took full responsibility for the kind of mom I wanted to be. Too often, I looked to Rob to solve problems that I had to solve myself. Sadly, I think there is a part of human behavior that looks for excuses when it comes to making choices for ourselves. I have certainly fallen into the trap of this kind of thinking. Primarily, this book is about what I learned in building relationships with my kids as a mom. Rob has his own relationships with each of our kids. Obviously, if Rob was writing this book, it would contain quite different wisdom from a dad's perspective.

Secondly, I have talked to women around the country and in different parts of the world who are either single moms or "feel alone" in their parenting. I wanted to write a book that would encourage and empower them as well. The faces of those moms and the memories of those conversations have inspired me to write this book. I want those women to know how much they can do for their children, even when they find themselves in unimaginable circumstances. I wanted to write something that communicated how valuable they are to their children, and to God. For every woman I have spoken with, I am confident that her voice represented at least another one thousand voices. I hope to reach those moms.

So, for both of these reasons, I write directly to moms. Of course, fathers are of equal importance and value to their children, so I hope my sweet husband Rob will soon write a similar book for dads!

Before I begin this journey into the heart of motherhood, I think it would be helpful if I introduce my children. It is through the lives and loves of these seven kids that I have learned the lessons that I am sharing in this book, so I think it is only appropriate that they are properly introduced. My firstborn is Robert William (RW) who is now 21 years old, a junior in college, playing baseball and studying architectural engineering. Then there is Elisabeth Jean (Lissy), age 19, who is a freshman in college, studying French, history and secondary education. She also loves dance, and has been speaking and writing with our family ministry. My third child is John Diehl (JD) who is 17 and a junior in high school. JD does a hybrid of homeschooling and traditional Christian education where he plays basketball and baseball. He also plays electric guitar to help his Mom with worship team at church. Marlayna Angenette (Laynie) is my fourth child, age 15, and a freshman in high school. She has a similar schooling situation as JD. She spends her extra time singing in musicals and on the worship team, and she loves being on the school dance team. Emily Margaret (Milly), age 11, is our fifth child and in fifth grade. She enjoys playing with her friends, basketball, dance and performing arts. She likes to smile a lot! Raeywen Marc (Ray), age 9, is my sixth child and in third grade. Ray enjoys life and just about everything he can get his hands on, especially LEGOs®, baseball and video games. Lucas Rush (Rush) is my seventh baby and he is five years old, He is completing his last year of preschool and he is eager to learn as much as he can. Hopefully, this gives you a glimpse of my life and my family. Many of the lessons I share in this book come from my experiences with these seven special people.

In my experience, I have found one thing every mom needs more of…joy! Joy in your heart and home will build the best relationships with your kids that you can imagine. The good news is that joy does not come from your circumstances. Joy comes from having a dynamic relationship with your heavenly Father that overflows into great relationships with your own children. And here is even more good news! Your heavenly Father does not demand perfection from you. In fact, He gives it to you through His Son, Jesus Christ. He does not need or want your perfect standards. He simply wants your heart. He wants to have a heart-connected, life-long relationship with you. He also wants you to have that kind of relationship with your children. That is what this book is all about.

If you want little or nothing to do with God or Jesus at this point in your life, I encourage you to continue reading here anyway. I cannot help but write about how Jesus has the most impact on who I am as a mother because He truly defines *who I a*m. However, I write this book to all moms, not just Christian moms. I have travelled the world speaking with and listening to many mothers. I know that moms share this in common: we desperately love our kids and desire to be the best mom we can be for our children.

Remember, today is a new day. Whether you are just beginning this journey of motherhood or a seasoned mom, today is an important day. Relationships with our kids are always changing because our kids change and we change. When you read this book, you may feel discouraged that the ideas are "too late" for you, but that is not true. In the present, we can always choose something new. We can choose new thoughts and let go of old mindsets. We can embrace our Father in Heaven who never changes and never gives up on His children. So as you read, open your heart to the new things God can do in you and through you as a mom.

> *Listen carefully, I am about to do a new thing,*
> *now it will spring forth; Will you not be aware of it?*
> Isaiah 43:19a (AMP)

⮞ *Part* 1 ⮜
Relationships are Key

Relationships are central for your children's success in life. You have a critical role to play in helping your children succeed relationally. Moms have so much influence in our children's lives in this area of relationships, if we truly understand how important we are!

Moms are extremely busy. Whether you are working inside or outside the home, have one child or several children, moms are actively involved in so many things. We are busy because our minds are occupied with the general welfare of other human beings.

After you become a mother, your mind is divided. Part of your mind will always be in "care" mode. We care for our children's physical, emotional, intellectual, social, and spiritual lives. There is not enough time in our day or room in our brains to care about all these things as well as we would like to. It is simply not possible. We have to make choices—and we learn by making mistakes.

Often, we have to get things wrong *before* we get things right. Yet as a mom, we really want to get as much right as possible the first time! We must keep two things in mind: we *will* make mistakes with our kids, and we can't do it all. The question is, what can we do?

What can we focus on that will help us even in the midst of all our mistakes? The answer is build relationships. Building healthy mom-child relationships is like creating a beautiful safety net for our families. All of us will make mistakes, hurt each other, and get things wrong. However, our goal is to stay connected and be there for each other through it all.

In this world of social media, cell phones, video games, and the internet, we see that real relationships are dying. This should not be the case in our homes. Moms, open your eyes in these next few chapters to see how important *you*—not what you do— but *you* are to your kids.

Chapter 1
What Every Mother Wants

Do you remember what it was like when you met your first child? Can you picture that initial moment? I can.

When the doctors laid my son RW in my arms, I remember an overwhelming feeling of love and joy. It was like nothing I had ever known before. Looking at my baby would fill my heart with joy, love, and happiness. These are the emotions of heaven.

Over the next few weeks, I was not only amazed with the love and joy for my child, but also keenly aware of the fragility of it all. RW's birth had been traumatic. My doctor came to see me the day after his delivery to pray with me. I did not even know she was a Christian. She was so shaken by the delivery, it was clear that she was thankful that Baby and Mom were going to be okay. I realized the joy and love that were overflowing in my heart would have disintegrated to despair and deep sorrow if Robert William had not survived the harrowing delivery. Joy was abundant, yet fragile.

It was then that God gave me a new thought, *Heaven is about permanent joy, unending love, secure peace, and overflowing happiness.* Who does not want that?

I thought of my beautiful friend, Beth, who had died from brain cancer when she was in 8th grade. I thought of her often. When I got married—which had been the best day of my life so far until the day RW was born—I remember feeling sad that Beth never got to experience getting married. Every time I thought of her, I had the same thought, *Beth got cheated from so much life.*

Now it was different. I held RW, my heart bursting with joy, love, and peace, and I thought of Beth again. Beth *has* experienced this joy—and far more—ever since she went home to be with her heavenly Father. Maybe she has not been cheated at all. Beth's joy is secure, permanent, and eternal.

A mother's love for her children is something that is too strong to be expressed with mere words. It is fierce, passionate, self-sacrificing, unyielding, comforting, joyful, and protective. A mother's love often outlasts all other earthly loves. I recently heard the testimony of a man who had been addicted to crack cocaine for over 30 years. Do you know the moment that broke him? It was the instant his mother told him not to call her anymore because she could do nothing to help him. He was broken because he knew his mother was the last person in the world who would ever turn him away. A mother's love will love until a mother's heart is broken.

All moms want to have love, joy, and happiness in our hearts and our homes. Love comes from relationships. Love comes from connection. The love you feel when you hold your baby in your arms comes from the connection you have with that baby. Your heart is immediately connected with that baby's heart. That connection started long before you held that baby in your arms, even from the moment of conception. And if you are a mother through adoption, you know that the heart connection you felt for your child began long before you held that child in your arms. Heart connection is the key ingredient to all good relationships.

We will be the most fulfilled as moms when we have heart-connected, life-long, discipleship relationships with our kids. Now maybe this description of a mother/child relationship sounds foreign to you. I get that. In this chapter you will get a clear picture of the type of close relationship I am describing. These kinds of relationships lead to more fulfilled, happy kids. Doesn't this phrase—happy kids—sound wonderful? I often say how thankful I am to have happy kids. All of us as moms want happy kids that grow into happy adults. The world needs more happy people.

Let me be really transparent here. When I was a mother of four young children, I was regularly entering the mom world of new pressures in my life. With each passing year for each child, new expectations were set before me. I also faced new questions, new developmental hurdles, and new challenges. *DAILY*, my mind was full of thoughts, "Are they doing ok", "Am I doing a good job", "Am I missing something important", "Am I messing my kids up", "what kind of home am I creating"....these are just a few examples. In the midst of all the the pressures, I noticed something. For the most part, my kids were happy. A day did not pass that was not filled with laughter, even if there had been a lot of tears and anger as well. I realized that I should not take this happiness for granted. I decided that I was not only extremely thankful that I had a happy, although very messy home, but that I also wanted to try to keep this happiness in my home. This decision gave a new perspective to all those daily pressures. How would these pressures affect my children's happiness? My eyes were opening to a very simple truth. Happiness is a good thing.

I have heard several sermons that draw a distinction between happiness and joy. Typically, the message is that happiness is a superficial emotion that depends on circumstances while joy is something that resides deep inside of us. Deep inner joy is an oxymoron. True joy is visible. We should be able to see it!

I would argue that happiness and joy are interchangeable terms— not distinctively different from one another. People who are filled with joy should be happy. And visible happiness is the only type of joy that kids will understand. Close relationships are closely connected to happiness.

So, what are "close" relationships? I would like to paint a picture of what my husband and I call heart-connected, life-long, discipleship relationships. This phrase gives a better description of a "close" relationship. Let me break this phrase down to explain it better.

Heart-connected: A heart-connected relationship is full of trust. It means that two people feel safe with one another. It means there can be honesty. It is a relationship where each person can be vulnerable about who they are, their faults, character flaws, and mistakes, and still feel loved. Heart-connection means we listen to each other and try to understand one another. It means we know a person is for us and never against us. This is true heart-connection.

Life-long: A mother-child relationship is intended to be life-long, not just until the child reaches adulthood. Our hope is for our children to be at our deathbed, or that we might be with them at their deathbed. Either way, the relationship we have with them is not weakened by age, distance, or life-circumstances. This does not mean we will see them or even speak to them every day as they become adults, but we will still have a heart-connected real relationship our whole lives.

Discipleship: This may be a word that is new to many moms. Everyone follows somebody or something. A disciple is a follower. Who or what do you want your kids to follow? I think it is clear that as Mom, we expect our kids to follow us. We desire for them to listen to us, obey us, to respect our words and our teaching. And why do we want our kids to follow us? It is because we love them more than anyone else on the planet (of course dads would be included in this as well). So, a discipleship relationship means we will train, discipline, instruct, and guide our kids into adulthood. We do not have peer relationships with our kids. The mother-child relationship is one defined by love, care, protection and discipline from the mother, and love, obedience, respect, and honor from the children. The only thing that changes over the course of the lifetime relationship is that once kids "own their life" they do not have to obey us. Once our kids are completely self-sufficient, they are independent and we cannot ask them to obey our demands. However, love, honor, and respect from our children will always be their part of the relationship just as love, care, and protection will always be our part of the relationship. Although the relationship with our children will never be that of a peer, this is not to say we do not develop "adult-to-adult" relationships with our kids. Rather, there remains a special, life-long connection between mother and child that is unique.

So why is it so important to have heart-connected, life-long, discipleship relationships with our kids? While most of this book will answer this question, I can give you one word that summarizes the answer: happiness.

Happiness is an underrated commodity in our culture but desperately sought for at the same time. In all the physical exams I have sat through with my seven kids, I have heard the nurses ask my children if they are depressed, but never if they are happy. Not being depressed and being happy are two quite different things.

Have you ever had the experience of traveling to an impoverished area of the world and working with people in those conditions? The feedback is almost universally the same: "The kids are so happy. The people are filled with joy, even though they have so little." These two words—happiness and joy—are what you often hear about when people go serve others in a third-world country. They see evidence that it is possible to have very little physical wealth but at the same time have great happiness and contentment.

In contrast, one can look at nations that have a high standard of living, with very little poverty in comparison to other parts of the world, and still find depression, anxiety, suicide, and despair. Wealth and physical comfort do not automatically create happiness and contentment.

What is the key ingredient to happiness? Relationships. Wherever you find authentic loving relationships, you will find happiness. When people are connected, they experience more joy. Loneliness and isolation breed sadness and depression. Heart-connected relationships breed happiness and joy.

The book *Training Children in Godliness*, by Rev. Jacob Abbott, dramatically changed my thinking about happiness. There is a chapter entitled, "Teaching Children to Be Happy." When was the last time you read anything on the subject of teaching children to be happy? I had never read anything on that topic, let alone a chapter in a book about how to train children. What was even more intriguing to me was that this book was written in 1890. If you ever want to get a fresh perspective about how to raise your kids, I highly recommend reading it.

While this chapter on happiness has many interesting points, I want to share some of Rev. Abbott's thoughts:

God intended for mankind to dwell in happy and loving union together. There is double enjoyment in family love: the pleasure of giving affection, and the pleasure of being the object of it. It is hard to tell which is the greatest. A man will sometimes neglect his family that he may increase more rapidly his wealth or influence in the world. However, he makes a sad mistake to barter his interest in some project, for the richer, deeper emotions of happiness which might be secured by loving and being loved by family members.[2]

Do not be confused that these words are addressed to men; that is simply because most books were addressed to men at this time. His words are timely for moms today.

What does every mother want? Happy kids. Maybe a lot of moms cannot even articulate this as a true desire. That is because we often do not realize what we want until it is gone. Most kids start out pretty happy, and it is often the ups and downs of life that have the potential to push the happiness out of our children.

Pressures of school success, teacher recognition, athletic performance, musical giftedness, and personal friendships all have a way of draining our children's joy. Having great successes for our kids can seem so important to us as moms until we start to see unhappy kids. When we see our kids struggle with emotions like depression, anxiety and sadness, success with all the "stuff" of life begins to lose its gleam. It is then we want the happiness back for our kids, but often discover how hard it is to recover.

Mom, do you realize that a strong relationship with you helps counter all of these ups and downs? Do you know that when your children experience safety, comfort, discipline, and heart connection with their mom, they navigate the challenges of life more successfully? A great relationship with you will serve as the best foundation for all the other relationships you want your kids to have in this life. Having a heart-connected, life-long, discipleship relationship should be your primary goal as a mom because relationships are the key to happiness. And I have no idea why it seems controversial to state this but here it is again: It is good to be happy.

It is worth a disclaimer here to clarify what I want to convey. I am not saying that if you have good relationships with your children that they will never be unhappy. All of us have emotional swings that may go up or down throughout the day. We are not talking about raising "Pollyanna kids" who are happy robots. What I am addressing is the deep need our kids have to be close to us. They need to know we are "for them," guiding them, training them, and understanding them. This kind of relationship with Mom builds resilience in children. Resilience enables us to withstand disappointment, failure, and even tragedy without these things dragging us into total devastation.

Why does it sound so shallow to say that one of your top goals as a mom is to raise happy children? I want happy children more than Division 1 athletes, National Merit® scholars, or Julliard musicians. Doesn't that take some of the mom pressure off? Praise God and thank Him every day if your kids are generally happy. That is something we as moms should never take for granted. It is a true blessing. If you are reading this and your children are struggling and unhappy, I want you to know that you can have a much greater influence in this area of their lives than you realize. Be patient with your kids, and more importantly be patient with yourself. Building heart-connected relationships with our kids takes time. Real relationships don't always look and feel happy. My point is that having real relationships will eventually lead to more happiness in our lives and the lives of our kids.

Every mom wants happy children. When we see our kids with happy hearts, we have happy hearts. We take great pleasure in our children's happiness. Likewise, our heavenly Father takes great pleasure in our happiness. God wants good for His children. We want good for our children. This is all very good, so let's embrace the mission of raising happy children.

 ## Mom Mission #1

Embrace your desire to raise happy kids.

Chapter 2
What's so Special about Mom?

The hand that rocks the cradle is the hand that rules the world - William Ross Wallace

I have grown into the meaning of this famous quote. When I first read it, I was intrigued. When I was a new mom, it intimidated me. Now I feel the truth of it. In my opinion, it is exactly what God intended.

Throughout history and virtually all cultures, it is the mother who rocks the cradle. Of course, this makes perfect sense because it is the mother who carries the child to life. She alone has the ability to feed her child with her own body. Have you ever considered that God did not have to create life in this fashion? He could have had our offspring born independent rather than dependent on us for nourishment. But in His grand plan, babies need their mothers in order to survive from the moment of their conception. While in modern society babies can now thrive even if they are not breastfed, historically that would not be true. Many babies would not have survived without their mother's milk. And whether a woman can breastfeed her baby or not is not the issue. The issue is that babies need their mothers. So, it only makes sense that it has been mothers—not fathers—who have held the primary responsibility of taking care of children throughout the ages, because God designed them for such a task.

Therefore, to say that the mother-child relationship is unique is an understatement. It is far more than unique. The relationship is sacred. Without your mother carrying you sacrificially in her body, you would not have been given life. Regardless of the kind of mother you may have had—kind or cruel—you received life from her. How often are we grateful to our own moms for that simple truth?

There are many lessons I have learned from having children and this one surprised me. Without going into gory details, I did not do pregnancy and childbirth easily. In fact, if I did go into the gory details, I can assure you that you would be completely shocked that I gave birth seven times. I experienced miracle upon miracle through many difficult pregnancies and deliveries.

In my first pregnancy, I suffered from morning sickness, heartburn, backache, foot pain, varicose veins, and stretch marks. I was so large that a woman asked me two times at my baby shower if I was having twins (true story)! I was miserable being pregnant. Many times, I questioned how much I really wanted to have children if this is what it required of me. The truth is, being pregnant is hard work—very hard work. It is hard physically and emotionally. Bringing children into the world is an act of self-sacrifice. So, while I lamented all of the things I hated about being pregnant, I was willing to endure the hardships because of the hope and joy of having a baby and welcoming the little one into my heart. It was during my first pregnancy that women who gave their babies up for adoption became new heroines in my thoughts. They are women of great courage and strength. I could not imagine going through all the pregnancy discomforts in order for someone else to have a baby. That is selfless love.

Having a baby changes your heart forever. While the trials of my first pregnancy were annoying, they were nothing compared to what I endured in my second pregnancy with my daughter Lissy. I was diagnosed with gallbladder disease that required immediate surgery followed by kidney stones and another hospital stay. I had morning sickness with RW, but was severely ill with Lissy, throwing up four to five times daily and even during the night. When I was told that I needed to have a surgery at seventeen weeks pregnant, I was surprised that the baby's welfare was my top concern. Somewhere between baby number one and baby number two I became a different person. Now it was baby first, me second. While the hardships were more threatening and scary during my pregnancy with Lissy, I endured them with more resolve and strength. I now *knew the joy of a new baby.* Having my son RW and not being able to imagine life without him gave me the courage to face new trials for the sake of a child I did not know. How can a woman love her unborn child so much that she is willing to risk her own life for the sake of a baby she has never met? This is sacred love. This is a mother's love. It is something worthy of honor.

Now I need to pause a moment to say that venerating a mother's love does not mean that I am diminishing a father's love. A father's love is also worthy of honor. But this is a book for moms—not for dads. The point of this chapter is not to state that the mother-child relationship is the only important relationship for children, but instead to honestly look at why the mother-child relationship is so unique. While fathers and caregivers are also indispensable in the lives of kids, that truth needs to be examined in a different book. Specifically, to the point of this chapter, fathers do not experience carrying and giving birth to children! Do I need to say any more? The mother-child relationship is special.

So, Moms, why is it that the hand that rocks the cradle is the hand that rules the world? It is because God has given all mothers great responsibility, great love, and great power to influence the hearts of their children. Mothers hold this sacred trust to care for their children.

Now, a few questions for you. Do you know you have such a high calling? Do you know how important you are to your children? How are you using the influence that God has given you as a mom to bless the hearts of your children? Have you seen this as a great responsibility and a great gift?

It may seem strange to look to the Bible for help in being a mom, but I realized I needed all the help I could get. I found much of that help by reading the Bible. The Bible helped me specifically in two ways. First, I began to see that the Bible is a record of how a perfect God, a Heavenly Father, deals with His imperfect children. Because I was aware of how imperfect I was, I knew raising "good kids" was going to be almost impossible. The Bible became my ultimate parenting manual. The best way to learn how to be a good parent was from a perfect Heavenly Father. Second, the Bible is full of imperfect people doing incredible things. So, if God has always used imperfect people to do great things, then why couldn't He use me to raise great kids? For these two reasons, I found myself studying the Bible to help me get this mom thing right.

There is a mom hero in the Bible who continues to stand out to me as a role model. It is not Mary the mother of Jesus, although I am sure she is a great role model for all of us. My heart is drawn to Jochebed, mother of Moses. This brave woman was a slave in ancient Egypt. When the Pharaoh issued a decree that all Hebrew baby boys were to be killed, Jochabed could not see her beautiful baby boy slaughtered. While risking her own life and the lives of her household, she hid Moses from the Egyptian authorities in order to protect him. She made a life raft and set her baby boy in the basket to float in the reeds by the banks of the Nile. Her desire was that he would be saved *even if* she could not have the pleasure of raising him herself (sounds like a heroic mom who gives up her baby for adoption). And then, God does more for Jochebed than she could ever imagine.

Not only is her son Moses saved from death, but he is adopted into Pharaoh's family. Yet, that is not the best part for Jochebed. Look at what happened when Pharaoh's daughter discovered the floating basket with the Baby Moses inside.

> When she opened it, she saw the child, and behold, the baby was crying. She took pity on him and said, "This is one of the Hebrews' children." Then his sister said to Pharaoh's daughter, "Shall I go and call you a nurse from the Hebrew women to nurse the child for you?" And Pharaoh's daughter said to her, "Go." So the girl went and called the child's mother. And Pharaoh's daughter said to her, "Take this child away and nurse him for me, and I will give you your wages." So the woman took the child and nursed him. When the child grew older, she brought him to Pharaoh's daughter, and he became her son. She named him Moses, "Because," she said, "I drew him out of the water." Exodus 2:6-10

So, Jochebed gets to nurse and raise her precious boy—knowing that he will one day be expected to live like an Egyptian, following Egyptian ways and worshipping Egyptian gods. The Bible does not give us a certain age when Moses left his mother and went to Pharaoh's daughter. Commentators suggest a range from as young as two[3] to as old as 12[4]. In my mind, I imagine a boy somewhere between the ages of three and five being escorted to the palace of Pharoah and saying goodbye to the only mother he had ever known. While Jochebed likely never saw Moses again, she held that boy's heart for his entire life.

Think about all that Jochebed must have taught Moses in those early years. Imagine the scene of Moses leaving the woman who had nurtured and loved him for the formative years of his life. I can see the tears of both mother and son.

My youngest son, Rush, just turned five years old. Since the age of three, every day—multiple times a day—he says, "Mom, I love you." I am the one he wants to start the day with each morning and I am the one he wants to end the day with each night. He "writes" me notes and gives me hearts. His face lights up when I walk into the room. He wants to show me everything. Rush wants me to be part of ALL that he is doing. This lesson is etched deep into his heart:

"Rush, do I love you a little or a lot?"

"A lot," he whispers.

Rush then adds again, "I just love you, Mommy."

Rush knows that his mommy loves him in a very special way. He knows that he loves his mommy. If Rush never saw me again, I have no doubt that he would continue to know my love. I do not think anything could wash away the imprint of my love on his heart.

Do you think anything could wash away the imprint of Jochebed's love on the heart of Moses? Apparently, even the wealth and power of the great kingdom of Egypt was no match for the mark of Jochebed's love on the heart of Moses. Long before Moses knows the Hebrew God or God's ways, he instinctively sided with the Hebrew people— his mother's people. When he saw a Hebrew slave being mistreated by an Egyptian, in his anger he killed the Egyptian. Even though he was raised in Pharaoh's palace, the heart of Moses was with the Hebrews. I wonder why? The hand that rocks the cradle holds the heart of the child.

Jochebed had a divine mission from God. Her son Moses became the leader of the Israelite people and one of the central figures of the

Old Testament. Yet she did not get to see the fruit of her obedience. God did not just choose Moses, He chose Jochebed as well.

One thing I like to repeat to all my children is this, "God must think that I am really special." When they ask why, I reply, "Because I get to be your mom."

This is the theme of the poem by William Ross Wallace that praises motherhood as the most powerful force of change in the world. One stanza within this poem, originally titled "What Rules the World," reads:

Woman, how divine your mission,
Here upon our natal sod;
Keep, oh, keep the young heart open
Always to the breath of God!
All true trophies of the ages
Are from mother-love impearled,
For the hand that rocks the cradle
Is the hand that rules the world.[5]

Your mother-love is a powerful force in this world. Are you starting to get a clearer picture of just how important *you* are to your children? You are a part of the divine mission of moms. Not the things you do, but simply *you*. The importance of who you are as a mom in your child's life is far more dependent on the relational connection you have with your child as opposed to your strengths and weaknesses as a person. You sacrifice every day for your kids because you love them and want what is best for them. You listen, advise, encourage, challenge and provide for them. That is what good mothers do. You are a good mom, not a perfect mom. Good moms can do great things and raise great—not perfect—kids. I have no doubt that any mom who reads a book about being a good mom has the desire and commitment to be a good mom!

Recently, my seventeen-year old son JD gave me a birthday card. I asked his permission to share part of what he wrote to me. While the whole letter meant so much to me, I was intrigued that my "negative" self-talk was the thing that he found annoying. I guess this should not surprise me. I am certainly annoyed when I hear my kids talking negatively about themselves. It should make sense that kids do not like hearing moms talk negatively about themselves. Our kids love us. They can often see all that we are doing well better than we can ourselves.

Moms, we have a divine mission. My heart is to share this truth with you because I want to encourage each of you not to live under the "bad-mom" shadow. The tears and time I wasted because of all the pressure I put on myself cannot be taken back. Too many moms are daily battling thoughts of discouragement and feelings of failure that simply have no basis in reality. Whether it comes from ourselves, our culture and community, our in-laws, our own parents, or even well-intended friends—many of us moms constantly feel we are letting down our families. Sadly, this kind of negative thinking can hurt the heart connection we have with our kids far more than our real faults, mistakes, and character flaws. Nothing positive comes from negative thinking. I will say that again, ***nothing positive comes from negative thinking.*** What we will learn in part two of this book is how our good desire to be great moms can turn into a destructive drive for perfectionism in ourselves and our kids that leads us down the path of negative thinking. And, ***nothing positive comes from negative thinking.*** Three times is a charm. [I really wanted to add an emoji here.]

Moms, we have a divine mission. You are a special mom. God has given you special kids. Your relationship with them is a special sacred trust—worthy of honor. That's a lot of specialness, but that is what is so special about Moms.

Mom Mission #2

Understand being a mom is a very special job given by God.

Chapter 3
Attachment, Attachment, Attachment

The greatest disease in the West today is not TB or leprosy; it is being unwanted, unloved, and uncared for. We can cure physical diseases with medicine, but the only cure for loneliness, despair, and hopelessness is love. There are many in the world who are dying for a piece of bread but there are many more dying for a little love. The poverty in the West is a different kind of poverty—it is not only a poverty of loneliness but also of spirituality. There's a hunger for love, and there is a hunger for God.

Mother Teresa, *A Simple Path*[6]

"This little one might make it. There is life in her eyes," Mother Theresa said when she picked up a tiny baby, not much bigger than her hands, from a crib filled with little ones. I will never forget a documentary about Mother Theresa that forever touched my heart. She was walking through her orphanage in Calcutta, India, where she ministered to the poor and desperate. In a crib there were several tiny babies all lying next to each other, almost like sardines. They were clean and dressed in pink and blue, having been rescued from the streets where they were left to die. Gently, Mother Theresa picked up the little one who had "life in her eyes." Then she acknowledged how they rescue the babies from the streets and take care of their physical needs, yet very few of them survive. Very few survive being unwanted.

The need to be wanted, loved, and touched is as vital to our well-being as food and shelter. We have a deep need to be accepted by someone—specifically our mothers. All of us desire to be wanted by our moms. God created mothers to be the original primary caregivers through breast-feeding. While breast-feeding is about naturally providing essential nutrition for babies, it is also the primary pathway for mother and child attachment. Of course not all moms breast-feed their babies. No matter which method of feeding is used, it is the foundational acceptance and care of the baby from the mother that allows a child to thrive.

I hope you can tell how important I believe *attachment* is when it comes to building great relationships with our kids. Before I begin, let me warn you against discouragement. As I address attachment, I will write a lot about babies and their need for healthy attachment with their moms. If you do not have a baby or have no plans to have any more babies, you may think none of this is relevant to you. Or, if you think that you made mistakes in this area, or your own mother may not have modeled loving attachment to you then you may falsely think the damage is irreversible. These negative thoughts are unproductive and untrue. My encouragement to you is to read this chapter with an open mind and an open heart. There will be lessons here that you can apply to whatever stage of mothering you may be in right now. They can also help you with future grandbabies!

I have been blessed to have a few close friends from Korea. I cannot tell you how much my parenting was influenced by these precious moms. While I love American culture, there is a Western tradition of individualism that I think works against us as moms. One way this individualism influences our thinking is the way we push our little ones to independence perhaps sooner than they are ready for it. Let me give you a clear example.

My Korean friends slept with their babies in their bedrooms, often even in their beds, not for the first month of the baby's life but the first three *years*. When I asked one of my friends about this difference in parenting, she explained that in Korea mothers keep their children close, so that their children can be independent from Mom when they are older.

When I asked her at what age in the traditional Korean culture do they begin emphasizing independence, she said around age twelve because they are now at an age when they can do more things without assistance. That age seemed so old to me! I recall feeling pressure from my parents to move my eight-week-old baby out of the bassinet in our room to the crib in the nursery! That would be unheard of in Korea where they believe a baby and a young child belong by the mother's side. In their culture the mother's attachment is valued as a precursor for her children's future health and success.

While attachment theory may have developed from Western psychologists such as Harry Harlow, John Bowlby, and Mary Ainsworth, many of their important conclusions have been self-evident throughout history and world cultures. John Bowlby, a British psychologist, emphasizes the importance of a secure and trusting mother-infant bond on development and well-being. He states that attachment "is what keeps a baby connected to his mother, considering the needs of the child that can only be satisfied by his parent."[7] It is almost exclusively the mothers who have had the charge of raising their own children throughout history in almost all cultures from ancient times until now. We do not need to be anthropologists to grasp that analysis, yet our current culture works against what historically has been best.

In fact, if you look at the original writings of attachment theorists such as Harlow, Bowlby and Ainsworth, you will find that the majority of their research revolved around the mother-child relationship. However, today if you read summaries of their work you will find all references to mothers have been changed to "primary caregivers." If you would like to research attachment theory on your own, I recommend that you look at the primary work of these psychologists as opposed to summaries you may find on the web.

God designed the mother-child relationship to be the foundational relationship for humanity. Attachment theory teaches us that children who are securely attached to their mothers, or surrogate mothers, will develop an "internal working model of a responsive, loving, reliable care-giver, and of a self that is worthy of love and attention and will bring these assumptions to bear on all other relationships."[8] I love the phrase at the end of this quote, "bear on all other relationships". What we are doing as moms and the love we give our children will *influence all the other relationships* in their lives. Mothers, including adoptive mothers, have this unique job to be a safe haven for their children, to teach them love and connection and dependability which anchors the rest of their future relationships.

While I may have learned about attachment theory in my psychology studies, I experienced the truth of this theory in my own home as a child with my own mom. I am blessed to have a mom who held the hearts of all three of her children. My mom used the God-given influence she had over her children to develop secure loving attachments with her kids. She was the one I ran to for safety, comfort, wisdom and hugs, lots of hugs. I had no doubt that my mother wanted me. When you are little, a loving mom is your safety net. My mom accepted us and that core acceptance from her gave me great confidence. I am not saying that I am never insecure, because that would not be true at all. I am saying that the love and acceptance I had from my mom gave me a core sense of value about who I was that stood strong even in the face of insecurities and personal rejection in relationships. She was, and continues to be, the heart of the home. As a grandmother of 15 grandchildren, she has played the most significant part in creating a family web of many heart-connected relationships. It is what she does best.

Have you ever met a person who is relationally-impaired? I am referring to a person who is not able to develop or maintain intimate personal relationships. I once knew a man who was married four times over the course of his lifetime and then lived with another woman before he passed away at the age of 90 years old. His pursuit of marriage and relationships obviously showed a desire to have success in this area. Sadly he faced disappointment time and time again. He kept a picture of his mother in the top drawer of his dresser. Yet he never knew his mother since she died at his birth from the flu epidemic of 1918. The first year of his life was spent in a hospital.

This man was William Rienow, my father-in-law. Rob and I once sent my father-in-law a book on attachment by Mary Ainsworth. We were hoping he might find some self-insight in his search for love. We do not know for certain if the book had any impact on his life. Rob can remember having breakfast with his dad and talking with him about how the loss of his mother had affected his life. While his dad quickly changed the subject, a tear immediately rolled down his cheek. At the age of 80, the heartache of the absence of a mother he had never known could not be hidden despite his best efforts.

Why is this so important for us to understand as moms today? Because attachment is what we have to begin with in order to have life-long, heart-connected, discipleship relationships with our kids. Attachment is simply the psychological term for heart connection. Heart connection is what we are building right away when we first hold our babies, cuddle them to sleep, and feed them. Clearly, God created these intimate ways of caring for our children that literally creates heart connection. Our children lie across our bosoms as we give them life, and the heart connection we make with them carries them throughout their lives.

Even though attachment is very important to a baby's overall health, attachment was not the main focus of any baby book I read as a new mom. My takeaway from the baby care books on the market was not the great need to develop a secure attachment with my children, but instead the importance of developmental milestones. Tragically, young moms are bombarded almost immediately after the birth of their children with lists of what their children "should" be doing at each month of their first year of life.

I can still recall the stress I had over the fact that my healthy baby boy could not roll over from his stomach to his back. He was "supposed" to do it by four months old which came and went. Still not happening at five months, six months, seven months, eight months, this new mom was getting more stressed that there was something deficient in RW's development.

Rob finally brought much-needed humor to my unnecessary anxiety about his development by stating, "I guess when RW is an adult he will fall on his stomach and simply not be capable of rolling over to his back. He will be helpless." After a lot of laughter, I realized my stress was completely manufactured by a developmental milestone list in that baby book. I still have not met one of those helpless adults, but I interact regularly with adults who are relationally impaired. Of course, there are developmental issues in our babies to which we should pay close attention. However, healthy attachment is also a critical issue. In fact, if you have a child with extra developmental needs, your heart connection is still a top priority, perhaps even more so.

I wish every baby book would address how essential it is for moms to develop a secure attachment to their baby! In my humble opinion, this is the most important thing that needs to happen in your child's first, second, third, fourth, and fifth years of life! Having a secure attachment, or heart-connection, with mom in the early years provides a healthy emotional foundation for our kids. This need in some ways far surpasses the physical developmental milestones list. It is the mom who needs to understand her baby's cries and meet her baby's needs and then grow to deeply connect with her child's emerging personality. It is Mom who needs to spend the most time with her baby, not all the time, but the majority of time. The baby needs to interact with a loving mother more than any other person. That is how secure attachment develops, and how heart connection is formed.

Babies need love, lots of love. While I have been emphasizing how important a mother's love and attachment is to a child's well-being, I am not excluding the importance of fathers, grandparents, siblings, or aunts and uncles in the life of a child. Sometimes there is no mother in the picture. Children who are loved and form attachments to family members who care for them will be able to thrive, but it is not the *ideal*. Babies want their mothers—simple as that.

There is one group of moms that is particularly well-educated about the importance of attachment—those who have adopted children. Every parent who enters a process of adoption has been taught the importance of developing a secure attachment with their adopted children. In fact, most often this training will include the need to keep the children only with their adoptive parents and immediate family, restricting the adoptive children from interacting with other people *until a secure attachment is formed with the adoptive parents.* It might be worth asking why similar wisdom is not regularly given to all new parents. I am not suggesting that it is necessary to restrict families with new babies from interacting with other close friends and extended family who also play key roles in forming loving attachment. However, I am suggesting that teaching new moms how to nurture a secure attachment with their new babies should be the primary focus of a good baby care book.

I once listened to a fantastic speaker who worked with adopted children and also had adopted multiple kids. She specialized in treating kids with RAD (reactive attachment disorder), which is a dreaded diagnosis in young children. It is often the precursor to a host of adult diagnoses such as personality and behavioral disorders. The speaker said that a lot of her conclusions and suggestions for preventing RAD in children were simply not politically correct, so she was not well-liked in the psychology world. It is not politically correct to say that mothers need to be the primary care givers of their children. That is why nurturing secure attachments may not be emphasized in typical parenting books.

Mother Teresa said, "We have not cured the disease of being unwanted." I think at the heart of a secure attachment is acceptance. Kids need to daily experience that they are accepted and wanted. They first want to be wanted by their moms. God designed their hearts to yearn for this type of unconditional love and acceptance from her. Children who have this are blessed. They are well-equipped to navigate the many life challenges they will face.

My heart behind this chapter is not to start some political cause but to talk with you heart to heart about this important issue. I want to encourage you to care less about all the standards and developmental milestones that you are bombarded with in the current culture and instead pour your heart into growing your "mom attachment" with your kids. While I will give you more specific suggestions in part three of this book, let me say here that this should be a daily goal. Each day is a new day and a new opportunity to build heart connection with your kids. Determine to elevate this as the mission you are best suited to fulfill. You can know your kids better than anyone else and you probably already do. Please do not get caught up in all the "shoulds" that your kids are supposed to be doing, especially if they detract from building heart connection. From that foundation, you can enjoy and pay attention to the typical developmental milestones. And then these milestones are helpful guides, which is what they are intended to be.

Moms, we all lead busy lives, but we can spend time with our kids to develop our connection as a safe haven for them. Attachment and acceptance go hand-in-hand to defeat loneliness and feeling unwanted. Isn't it encouraging to realize that the relationship you have with your kids can anchor them to have meaningful future relationships with friends, future spouses, and their future children? So, let me encourage you to make heart-connection and attachment a top priority in your home.

 Mom Mission #3

Make heart-connections with your kids important in everyday life.

Chapter 4
Raising People, Not Products

I am a homeschooling mom. That was not my plan, but it has been my path.

Homeschooling has been an interesting, challenging, and rewarding journey filled with ups and downs. However, what I never expected was how much this journey would teach me. The lessons I have learned are endless! In this chapter I will share one example with you that has been so important to me.

In my early years of homeschooling, I was often stressed about whether my kids were meeting all the academic standards at each grade level. And when you are in charge of the education of your kids as well as managing the cooking, cleaning, clothing, activities, and friendships for your entire household—you end up going a little crazy! Well, a lot crazy is much more accurate. Of course, above these duties as Mom, I am also a pastor's wife—a big job in itself.

So, quite frequently if not always, there was not even one area of my life where I felt I was managing things successfully. This included taking care of myself. After my third and fourth babies, I began experiencing health problems due to the toll of difficult pregnancies and challenging deliveries.

I began to feel like—and say—that I was a "lemon." I am not sure if people use this term anymore, but it usually refers to a car that has continual problems. My first car was a lemon. I remember the rearview mirror coming off when I tried to adjust it. I was just sixteen and, honestly, not a very good driver. I definitely had no business driving a car without a rearview mirror. But off I went to school—

determined to enjoy having a car. Regardless of its ongoing problems, I could handle a lemon type of car.

But now *I* was the lemon. This, I could not handle. As I got through one health challenge, there was another just around the corner. I kept thinking that if God just made me a better and stronger version of me, then I could master all of it. While this way of thinking was completely unproductive and untrue, it did make me reorder my priorities. I could not be successful at it all, at least according to the standards I was setting for myself. I had to choose daily what was going to get the best of my attention and energy.

We have a heavenly Father who is a good parent. He gently leads us—even when we have faulty thinking and misguided ideas. In Isaiah 40:11, God says that He will *gently lead those who have young.* I clung to the truth of that verse. I was willing to be gently led. I was willing to accept my shortcomings and hear the voice of my good Father who was not trying to fix me but guide me to a better way of mothering.

Adding to my stress level at this time in my life, I was working part-time as a marriage and family therapist. I worked because we needed the money. I was married to a youth pastor and we had major student debt along with a growing family.

In my counseling sessions, I noticed a pattern in all of my clients that stood out to me. The vast majority of them, regardless of age, were dealing with some level of hurt and pain that they carried from their relationships with their parents. Usually in the first session—but almost certainly by the second—I would be processing with my clients what might be called "mom and dad wounds."

This "pattern" was not limited to the people I saw professionally, but also to the student families I worked with in youth ministry. I knew the parents of these students and they were wonderful people who had my respect. Yet, many of the girls I met with had struggles with their parents, especially their moms. At the same time, I was personally working through issues that I had with my own mother. Whether we have wonderful or not-so-wonderful moms, none of us are raised by perfect people. We ALL have to process the good and bad parts of the relationships we have with our own mothers.

I noticed an important pattern. I realized that none of the people who came to me for counseling were seeking help because they had trouble spelling, low ACT scores, struggles with math, or problems with athletics, abilities or musical talent. In fact, these types of problems were non-existent in adulthood. So, as God helped me put two and two together, I became aware that so many of the pressures that plagued my daily mom-life were not the things that were going to cause real problems in adulthood. In fact, the truth was quite the opposite. Many of the important things I was prioritizing as a mom were casting shadows over the *most* important things.

As God cleared those big shadows, I began to see that what my kids will need most from me is a healthy relationship *with* me! I began to ponder, what if instead of talking to therapists and youth pastor's wives when my kids are older about the hurts they have from me, maybe they could simply talk *to* me? Maybe I could start building a relationship with them that will bless them in such a way that it will have a far greater impact than any amount of academic, social, athletic, or musical success. What if my kids wanted to talk with me about their problems because they are certain that I know them best, love them with all my heart, and will not forsake them?

We Are Raising People—Not Products

For the Children's Sake by Susan Schaeffer Macauley, is one of the best books on parenting I have ever read. Macauley teaches something in this book that has transformed me as a mom. It is simply this, "Children are born persons." Read this carefully in her own words:

> Try a simple experiment. Take a small child on your knee. Respect him. Do not see him as something to prune, form, or mold. This is an individual who thinks, acts, and feels. He is a separate human being whose strength lies in who he is, not in who he will become... Look well at the child on your knee. In whatever condition you find him, look with reverence. We can only love and serve him and be his friend. We cannot own him. He is not ours.[9]

Is this not beautiful? Our children are valuable right now at whatever developmental stage they are at, and with whatever skills they have. Do we look at our children as people who need be formed and molded, or with reverence?

Reverence is not a word we often hear in our current culture. In fact, it might be said that in America today there is a culture of irreverence. According to the Webster 1828 dictionary (which is my favorite dictionary by the way) reverence is defined as fear mingled with respect and esteem: veneration. So, looking at our kids with reverence is like saying to ourselves "I am amazed at who you are, and I respect who you are, and I am in awe that I get to be your mom."

When I first read this, on one level I intrinsically believed this and operated on this truth. But when I was honest with myself, I realized how easy it was to slip into what I now refer to as a "product mentality." This is the mindset that it is my job as Mom to make sure my children reach their full potential and maximize their gifts so by the time they graduate high school, they have an impressive list of accomplishments. They need to be stand-outs. I need to raise the 18-year-old super kid who can win the awards and the scholarships. Oh, and in order to do this I have to start early. I have to prioritize the right activities, schools, friends, and opportunities so that my kids have the best chances to achieve success.

It sounds exhausting to read that list, but it is what many moms continually feel and believe. If you secretly carry the weight of these expectations, I can assure you it is no secret to your kids. When we have a product mentality, we cannot help but pass that mentality on to our family. Your kids can feel as exhausted with it as you do.

Of course, being a homeschool mom, I was far more enlightened. I was determined to not fall into the standard cultural traps. I was not going to allow my children's value to fluctuate with standardized testing results or their spot on the elite sports team. I was far too noble for that. Instead, I had a list that involved character qualities and spiritual knowledge. I certainly hope you can read my sarcasm. Sadly, this leads to a different version of the product mentality—"the super-Christian kid." It is still focused on the product I am raising more than the person I am parenting.

I became aware of this one night when I was putting my daughter Lissy to bed when she was about six years old. I would often ask my kids, "Do you know I love you?" The answer from all of them was always, "Yes." Yet this night, I followed up with a different question. I asked Lissy, "Do you know I am proud of you?" The answer was, "No."

Lissy needed a little more "Susan Schaeffer Macauley" in my mothering. She needed to know I valued her for who she was at the moment, not for what she was becoming. Thankfully, I was learning to listen to the voice of the Good Shepherd guiding me despite all of my shortcomings. I was of value to God not for who I needed to become but for who I was right now. I needed that message. Lissy needed that message. Do you and your kids need this truth? It is never too late to receive that good news for yourself and to give that good news to your precious kids. You are valued by God for who you are right now, not just for who you are becoming.

I did not need Lissy to explain her answer to me. I instinctively knew why the answer was no. You see, whether or not my list was noble or superficial was not the problem. The problem was that I had let my desire for her to meet the standards I was setting overshadow the value of my relationship with her. When a child is continually corrected for her shortcomings, it is very difficult to feel her mom's approval.

After having a compliant firstborn son, I was not prepared to parent a strong-willed but sensitive and timid daughter. My standards were crushing her spirit and, even worse, fraying our mother-daughter relationship. If I wanted her to come to me to talk about her problems when she was in high school, then I needed to build a healthy relationship while she was young. That needed to be the number one goal.

Raising people rather than "products" will necessarily involve the need for healthy relationships because people are relational creatures. In all the spheres where we live and work, we need to be able to have good, healthy relationships. This will determine our kids' future life success more than their personal achievements. We literally need other people for health and happiness. Raising our kids to be truly successful adults will require us, as moms, to focus on teaching them how to have healthy relationships with others. The good news is that we can have a tremendous influence on our children if we keep this goal at the forefront.

When we keep our top focus as moms on building life-long, heart-connected discipleship relationships with our kids, we are turning our hearts to our most important "Mom Mission." We are operating in our special God-given role, and we have the capacity for excellence! It is not overwhelming or mission-impossible. Instead, it is an essential Mom Mission.

Mom Mission #4

Focus on raising a person, not a product.

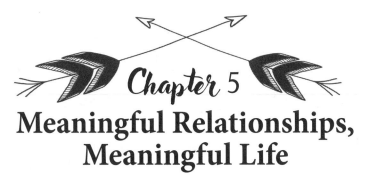

Chapter 5
Meaningful Relationships, Meaningful Life

Every Christmas our family will watch *It's a Wonderful Life*, the famous Frank Capra film about George Bailey. George thinks he is a failure because his life dreams of leaving the small town he grew up in to travel and impact the world have not come true. When George—in a moment of despair—is considering suicide as a viable option, he is visited by a "not-so-perfect" angel named Clarence, who leads him on a journey. This reveals to George that his single life has had an impact beyond what he could imagine. George begins to see how his life is abundantly "rich" because he has invested himself in his family, friends, and community. At the end of the movie, Clarence leaves a message for George in a book that reads, "No man is a failure who has friends."

Often, I think of myself as a "George Bailey-type." Despite my desire to move to Texas since I was a young girl, I have lived in the same town my whole life, even attending the same church until I was 41 years old. My kids have grown accustomed to me running into people around town and starting in-depth conversations. When they ask me, "Mom, who was that?" it is fun to answer, "Oh that was my best friend in junior high" or, "she was an amazing student leader in our youth group," or, "we were friends in second grade." Living a lifetime in the same town has given me a unique perspective about the value of people in my life. While I still pine at times to live in the Lone Star State, I feel abundantly blessed to have so many relationships in my life that have been dear over many, many years.

However, when I think of Clarence's words to George Bailey at the end of that movie, I have pondered if someone is a failure who has no friends? Now failure is a strong word and one that most of us dare not use. I do not think that I have ever referred to someone as a failure. God does not look at His children and see failure. God sees hope. What do you see? What do you see when you look at others? Your kids? Yourself?

Yet the sad truth is that many people *feel* like failures. They have come to the same place as George Bailey—at the edge of their own bridge. It is an overwhelming sense of despair and loneliness, and there has not been a "Clarence" to point the way to truth. And even if a "Clarence" did show up, there may not be a lot of meaningful relationships in their lives.

In our current culture of expediency and social media, meaningful relationships with family, friends, and our communities have been slowly dying. **People *feel* like failures when they have no friends.**

In fact, did you know that loneliness is an emerging public health threat? In a recent article published in *The Hill,* new studies are finding that loneliness is a risk factor for several other health problems such as obesity, decreased resistance to infection, depression, and dementia. This article also reported that "Gen Z appears more prone to experiencing significant loneliness. Gen Z (22 years and younger) may be the loneliest generation."[10] These studies also found that adolescents who spent more time on social media and devices such as smartphones were more likely to report mental health issues.

My oldest son, RW, is 21 and is the beginning of the Gen Z generation. I can still remember an extremely interesting conversation we had when he was a junior in high school. While we continued to homeschool, RW had the privilege of attending a school part-time. This school emphasizes the importance of relationships in quality education. Being there only part-time, RW often felt like an outsider looking in even though he was certainly accepted as part of the community by his peers and teachers. However, he did not quite know how to fit into the daily system of the school.

He came home one day and said to me, "Mom, I finally figured out this school thing. These kids go to school every day, sit in class, meet the same people in halls between classes to share what is on their phones with each other. Then they sit at lunch with their phones on doing the same thing, then after school they go to their other activities. They go home, maybe have dinner with their family, do homework, go to bed, and then do the same thing the next day and the next. So instead of building relationships with each other at school, they are more like information booths just sharing information back and forth, and they have no time to invest in relationships with the people who know them best—like their parents and siblings. So, while the school emphasizes relationship-building, I wonder how much relationship-building is actually happening."

When your 16-year-old son says something like that, trust me as a mom, you pay attention! First of all, I do not want to imply anything negative about the school and its mission of excellence in relationships. The focus of the school is exceptional and many students find life-long friendships with peers and teachers from the school because of their unique approach to education. But what I was seeing and learning as I watched my kids in high school is that in our current culture, we cannot *depend* on institutions—even when they are excellent—to teach our children how to have quality, meaningful friendships. Relationship-building skills start in the home. Moms play a key role in teaching their kids these skills.

We live in the age of delegation parenting and sadly it starts very early. We can too easily reduce our impact as moms to simply getting our kids into the "right" institutions. From the "right" daycare, to the "right" preschool, to the "right" elementary school, all the way up to the "right" college. There is no "right" institution that will ever replace the value of your relationship with your own child! *You, Mom, will teach life lessons to your children that will impact their lives far more than any school.*

I need to stop and ask whether you believe that. Do you understand how important you are to the future success of your kids? It is not about how spectacular you are as a mom, but how much you embrace the importance of your job as a mom. It is not just about attaching to our babies when they are little but staying attached as well! We need to stay connected, stay involved and pursue heart-connected discipleship relationships with our kids so that we can help them develop other meaningful relationships.

It is easy to be deceived by thinking good relationships with our children means conflict-free, easy relationships. Nothing could be further from the truth. Good, strong relationships are inherently messy.

The school my children attend have in their mission statement "Excellence in relationships." That sounds beautiful. How would you describe an excellent relationship? On the surface an excellent relationship sounds like something peaceful, supportive, encouraging, loving, and stress-free.

But let me give you a different definition of an excellent relationship. It is a relationship that survives angry outbursts, selfishness, envy, hostility, and disappointment. A relationship that is committed through the mountain tops of life as well as the valleys. A relationship that is full of grace and full of truth. A relationship that can handle individual differences, personality quirks, bad habits and character flaws with mercy that overflows. A relationship that is characterized by real love, not just warm feelings. We typically have few excellent relationships in our lives because, honestly, we are not capable of having relationships like this with that many people. Excellent relationships exist primarily in family and close friendships. God designed us to desire excellent relationships.

The type of relationship our kids need to experience starts with us. I think you are demonstrating "excellence in relationships" when you can look your child in the eyes and tell him that you love him even after his impulsivity and anger has literally wrecked your day. It is "excellent" when you can endure your teenager's selfish behavior, blow up in anger, admit that you should not have lost your temper, try to deliver an effective consequence, and then face the same problem the next day or in the next twenty minutes. But you are there. You are not giving up. You are the mom that is loving when love looks ugly. That is "excellence in relationships." Your kids will learn from you.

Most moms I know love their kids excellently. They love through the tempers, the selfishness, and the disappointments. They are committed to their kids in the good times and the bad. Their relationships with their children are characterized by real love, not just warm, fuzzy feelings. But these moms may not recognize that what they are doing is the *best* gift they are giving their kids—an important springboard for all other relationships in life!

It is too easy for us as moms to miss the forest for the trees. When we love our children with excellence, we are blessing them with the forest—with abundance. So many kids in this world never get that kind of love from any mom. I can see Mother Teresa holding those precious abandoned babies. We can only wonder what the sad circumstances were that led to moms discarding their babies on the street. Yes, many kids do not have the blessing of a mother's love. But my guess is that if you are a mom taking the time to read a book about mothering, then you already love your kids out of this world. You do not need a book to tell you to love your kids. You need a warning though: ***do not get stuck in the trees!***

Do not get consumed by all the things you think your kids need to have in order to have success in life. Don't think that you are messing them up if you are not feeding them the best diet, or getting them in the right activities, or hitting every important milestone. Trees hit us at every stage of parenting. It is like we make it through one tricky obstacle course only to find ourselves in the middle of another one.

For example, I had no idea the effect high school standardized testing was going to have on my kids. My oldest son RW had always been an excellent student; his academic success was not a tree I ever got stuck on because that part for him always came easy. But his first ACT® score threw him for a loop. I am not even going to mention the score, but let's just say it was lower than his standards—or what we were expecting. Needless to say, all of a sudden, he thought he was not smart. It shocked me how one score could alter his view of himself in an area of great strength. But this started me down the negative mom path, thinking that I had really messed up, too. I told myself, "I should have been doing a much better job of making sure he was prepared for these tests." That part might be all true, but the ACT® test is still just a tree. At the end of the day, RW's success as a person will have nothing to do with that score.

Moms, we *are daily* bombarded. We are bombarded with all the things we are told are essential in order for our kids to be successful. We can let ourselves get so caught up in it that it has a very negative effect on our relationship with our own kids.

So many of the obstacles we face in our parenting are the trees. It is not that we should ignore the trees, but we can't get stuck in the trees. When we get stuck, our kids will too. All of a sudden, the not-so-important things will become the all-consuming things, and then we are in danger of losing the forest.

If we can love our kids well, if we can strive to develop excellent relationships with them, then we can teach them to love well and to strive to have excellent relationships with others. We are then truly preparing our kids for success. "No man is a failure who has friends."

This is what I teach my children about friendship. I tell them to seek out one friend who they know has their back, who they can count on not to bad-mouth them, who they know will always welcome them at the lunch table, who will stand up for them in a crowd. If they have one friend like this, then they should consider themselves abundantly blessed. Unfortunately, many people go through their whole lives never having this kind of friend.

And moms, if we are our kids only true friends, even for a season, our kids are still abundantly blessed. There are far too many souls in this world that never experience excellent love, but moms can naturally fill that gap. Let us determine to build excellent real relationships with our kids so they will not only live well, but love well.

When we enter into part two of this book, we will take a closer look at the factors that can have a negative effect on building excellent relationships with our kids. You will be surprised that even a small shift in our thinking and expectations can have a big impact in our families!

 Mom Mission # 5

Remember real relationships with your kids will help them have success in life.

≫ *Part* 2 ≪
Perfectionism Kills Relationships

Relationships are not easy. In our current culture, we see the drive and need for authentic connection and community, while at the same time, many people lack the life skills they need to build healthy relationships. We see that family brokenness is at the heart of community disconnection. Many of us have the skills to be friendly, connect with people on a superficial level, and even have a cordial, "close" friendship. These skills are quite different from the skills needed to maintain deep loving relationships with spouses, friends, and family. It is in these close relationships that our needs for intimacy are met. I would say all of us know the feeling of being in a room full of people while still feeling lonely and isolated. Similarly, this world is full of people with crowded lives full of people with whom they share no meaningful heart-connected relationships. Many of us live isolated lives full of people.

You may feel as a mom you struggle with having close relationships. You may be disconnected from your own family or have few close friends. If so, you are certainly not alone. I believe most of us can feel that way, whether it is all the time or only some of the time. Building healthy heart-connected relationships takes work, time, energy, and humility. The process of acquiring humility is not a fun process. However, we have a head start if we are a mom! Being a mom is a role well suited for learning humility—if we want to learn it. Even if you feel that you are no rock star when it comes to having good personal relationships, you can learn to have awesome relationships with your kids. You will best do this by abandoning perfectionism and embracing humility. Easy to say, difficult to do, something we all can achieve.

Chapter 6
I am Not a Perfectionist!

"Amy, I just love coming over to your house because you are *just so real.*" I had three people say this to me in the course of a month. My internal translation of this statement, "Amy, I am amazed you are willing to have people over with your house being such a mess."

Yes, I just love "being real." The honest reality is that I was not "choosing" to be real. I would have much preferred to have my house look beautiful and orderly like my dear friend's house next door. I believed there was something seriously wrong with me because I was not able to keep it all together in my home or (generally) in my life! No, this was not a proactive decision; I felt forced into "being real."

Becoming a mother and having four babies in six years was like taking a humility pill that my body wanted to reject. I had not in any way mastered housekeeping, married life, ministry life, and work life when motherhood landed on me as well. All of a sudden, I had so many new responsibilities that I could not manage according to my own standards. However, other people's standards and expectations also led me to conclude that I was falling short in my many roles.

So, there was no way I would have viewed myself as a perfectionist. I knew perfectionists and I certainly was not one! Perfectionists had perfect houses, perfect schedules, perfect figures, and dressed themselves, their kids, and even their husbands perfectly. This in no way described my life, in my humble opinion. For example, perfect mothers do not forget to pick up their neighbor's kids at preschool. This happened more than once, but thankfully each time to different neighbors. If it makes any difference, I also once left my own sweet daughter, Laynie, at home. At least my absent-mindedness is not limited to other people's kids. I'm not so perfect, right?

Isn't it funny the things you learn about yourself when you are desperate for help. When I learned about the "Flylady," the home organization guru, I was just trying to get help on how to manage my home without going insane. Yet it was because of these every-day problems, I learned some very important lessons *about myself* in those first scattered ten years of family life. Out of my desperation, I found the book *Sink Reflections* by Marla Cilley the Flylady. Her approach to home management was life-changing for me in so many ways. Read it in her own words:

> Do you hear your Mother's or Whoever's voice saying, "That's not good enough, you can do better than that. Go back and do it right!" It really did not matter how nice a spin they put on it. The message came through loud and clear: "Anything less than perfect is unacceptable!" And the horrible exten-sion: "Unless you are perfect, you are not good enough" Or "Not Worthy of Being Loved!!!"[11]

I had self-diagnosed my perfectionist problem. To my surprise, those thoughts were rattling around my brain! Although I would not have said it to anyone, including Rob, that I thought I needed to be perfect to be loved, deep down inside that was what I believed. A de-sire to be perfect was leaving me unsettled and dissatisfied with many areas of my life. It was also preventing me from action. Because if you do not think you can make things perfect, you often stop trying.

Perfection is an unrealistic and unattainable standard we place on ourselves and others. Perfectionism is best described as a hid-den drive that leaves us unsettled because things are not going the way we imagine they should be. Most of us desire perfection. In fact, it is a drive for heaven. Therefore, it is not wrong to desire perfection (heaven), but it is when we expect, demand, try to create, and strive for human perfection that we get ourselves into a lot of trouble!

I remember when I became convinced of my hidden perfection-ism (hidden to me that is). The revelation became even more clear through understanding the hurt that this was causing in the relation-ships with my husband and my kids.

We have a large wall in our family room that is too big for an entertainment center; so, we created a gallery wall of art instead. Our gallery wall is filled with pictures of friends, family and meaningful pieces of art. Because we were on a tight time schedule to complete the project before my daughter Lissy's graduation party, we hung the pictures but never used Command™ strips in order to keep them perfectly in place. That was in the spring of 2017. You might ask if I ever got around to completing the project the way I intended. (If you notice, the pronoun switched to *I* and not *we* since it is I who am the only one who feels the need to get the pictures perfectly placed.) Consequently, I regularly sit in the room looking at the crooked pictures.

One morning when I was reading my Bible, I looked up and saw the myriad of crooked picture frames on the wall and felt the same frustration at myself for not getting the project done to perfection. The Holy Spirit spoke this to my heart, "Amy, you should be looking at what is in the picture frames." As I looked up at the wall again, tears started to flow. So many faces of people I care about, so many memories, and so much love is all over that wall in crooked picture frames. I get to choose what I am going to look at each day.

Our lives are lived in crooked picture frames. Every time I am adjusting myself to compensate for one problem, another one is creeping up around the corner. My eleven-year-old daughter Milly is extremely resilient, which is something about her personality that amazes me. She can endure rejection and hurt from her peers and it does not seem to create much stress in her life. In fact, she can even be happy in the midst of those types of trials. However, she can be brought to tears quickly when her mother continues to point out what she is doing wrong without praising all that she is doing right. Am I really looking at her, or just regularly adjusting her picture frame? Milly knows when I *see her.*

Learning to *see* my children without always adjusting the picture frame was an important part of the humility pill I needed to take as a mom. I am forever grateful to the Flylady for opening my eyes to my deep, ingrained spirit of perfectionism. I had no idea how much this was negatively affecting my view of myself, my husband, and my kids. It was not just about my house, which was the main purpose I read the Flylady book. It was about me. Feeling unsettled and negative about not reaching standards was robbing me of joy! Sometimes the standards came from culture, sometimes from women in my community, sometimes from family, sometimes from my husband, but most often from myself. No matter where the standards came from, I always had the choice to accept them or not accept them.

My first lesson was to learn that perfection was not possible. It was not possible for me to "fix" everything. I could not "fix" my house, my husband, my kids, or myself. For example, I could spend days organizing a room in my home and get it to my standard of perfection, but at the same time another room needed my attention. Someday when I am no longer raising seven children and homeschooling, I will be able to focus on my home in such a way that I can keep it "fixed." However, people and relationships are always going to be in some state of imperfection. I can't parent every negative thing I do not like out of my kids just like I certainly can't parent everything I do not like out of myself or out of my husband. I have to learn to accept and even enjoy all the imperfections.

Imperfection is the reality of the world we live in every day. In fact, God Himself does not expect perfection. That is why He needed to send His Son Jesus into the world. I cannot be made perfect by my own willpower and neither can you. If God does not expect perfection, why do we?

While I was self-diagnosing, I do not think my husband, my parents or even my young kids were at all surprised. A drive for perfection, whether spoken or unspoken, will lead to a spirit of discontent. And when we have high standards for ourselves, this naturally overflows to everyone who is in close relationship with us. While I cannot remember how frequently Rob put words to his feelings, I know he would often feel like a failure in our home. It pains me to write this but I have to be honest. If I had not changed course early in my mothering, I am sure my kids would have often felt the same way. You cannot have a life-long, heart-connected relationship with someone if they feel like a failure when they are with you. It's just not possible.

Perfectionism kills relationships. It is what happens when unrealistic standards invade our relationships. Therefore, it is too soft to say that perfectionism can hurt relationships. It literally kills them over time.

I am not saying that perfectionism is the only thing that kills heart-connection with our kids. Abandonment, abuse and immorality are some relationship killers that certainly affect many children around the world. However, I think a spirit of perfectionism is a deceptive relationship killer that sadly affects many well-intentioned, loving moms—those who would never abuse or abandon their kids. Take an honest look at yourself and ask if a spirit of perfectionism is having a negative effect on you being the best mom you can be. Is it working against you as you strive to have life-long, heart-connected relationships with your kids?

As we keep diving into the deceptive pool of perfectionism, I hope this next chapter will help you trade a drive for flawlessness for a heart of rest. A humble heart that sees beauty in our imperfections will see the perfection of God more clearly. A humble heart is a grateful heart, and a grateful heart is a happy heart. Happy mom hearts can bring lots of needed happiness into many homes.

Mom Mission #6

Choose humility over perfectionism.

Chapter 7

The Good-Enough Mom

"So, what are your strengths?" It was a simple question and one I should have been able to easily answer.

Sitting at a baseball game, I was having an interesting conversation with an amazing single mom—also a business woman in the workforce—who is raising three kids. She asked me again, "What are your strengths?"

My brain sort of just stalled and went blank. Nothing came to mind. I was quiet. Me, quiet? Having nothing to say in a conversation? I assure you, this does not happen often. But that day it did. I sort of laughed it off, with a quiet giggle, and said, "I am not sure."

She pressed harder, "Everyone has strengths." That is true. I knew I had them. I knew I was not a miserable mom. I was raising great kids. Something must be going right. Why couldn't I name any strengths?

There was a simple answer that I reflected on during my long drive back from the baseball tournament. *I was obsessed with my weaknesses.* If that mom had asked me about my weaknesses, I could have talked forever. Trust me, there would have been an easy flow of conversation and analysis. But my strengths? I had not thought about my strengths because I had forgotten about them.

Sadly, my brain was hyper-focused on all the wrong things. I knew I could be doing better, both as a mom and as a wife. No matter how much was going right in my home and with my kids, I had a long list of things that needed to change. For example, I needed to be more organized, cook healthier meals, get up early and go to the gym, be more frugal, read more to the kids, etc. These were just some of the thoughts that would occupy my mind most days. That was just the mom list. There were also mental lists of how I could be a better wife, daughter, daughter-in-law, sister, and friend. There was also the pastor's wife list and the professional list. I could be doing much more with my degree and my gifts in the area of dance and music. Even writing all of this out is exhausting, and frankly a little embarrassing.

Perfectionism kills. It kills a lot of things. One thing it kills is joy. Another is gratitude. Gratitude and joy go hand in hand. Without gratitude, you will not have joy which we all desire. When you are under the cloud of the unconscious, subtle (or not so subtle) drive of perfectionism, you cannot *see* all that you have to be grateful for in *yourself*. You cannot be thankful for *your God-given strengths* (yes— you do have strengths).

Remember I said that I went through a phase of believing I was a lemon. My distorted view of myself had a lot to do with the fact that my pregnancies and deliveries were more often difficult and complicated. One of the biggest trials I went through was almost losing my life and the life of my baby in my sixth pregnancy. Without going into the ugly details, I had a placenta abruption two weeks before my due date with my son, Ray. I am so thankful that we are both here today. I was told that Ray was born completely blue due to the lack of oxygen, even though once the doctors discovered that they were losing him and me, it took them only eight minutes to get Ray out of me. Within five minutes after his birth, Raeywen Marc's Apgar test went from a four to a nine. All I remember is being rushed into the operating room and then the next voice I heard was, "well you have a beautiful baby boy and judging by the size of you I do not know how he fit in there." Like almost all of my kids, Ray was big, nine pounds and one ounce, two weeks early!

Needless to say, the road to recovery was difficult for both Ray and me. After going home from the hospital with Ray, I was rushed back in the same night for a blood transfusion. While I do have fair skin, my color was literally white. However, it was this time in my life that God taught me that my *perceived* weakness was actually revealing my *real* strength. I will never forget sitting in the room with my family doctor at Ray's six-week check-up, fighting back tears, asking my doctor, "why did the placenta abruption happen?" My mindset was, "what is wrong with me; what is wrong with my body?"

My doctor blessed me that day with a wonderful lesson that I now want to pass on to you. He told me that while he was growing up on a farm in Iowa, he had to build a lot of fences that required strong fence posts. He said that the only way they could measure the strength of the fencepost was by the strength of the storm that the fencepost could handle. With each passing storm, they would know how strong the fenceposts were. There was really no other way to measure the quality of the fenceposts *except* seeing how well the posts stood in the storm. My doctor then looked into my eyes, which were beginning to fill with tears, and said something like this, "Amy, your body just survived a tornado, and Ray just survived a tornado. In fact, others may not have survived what you both just endured. Amy, you are a very strong, healthy woman and you have a very strong, healthy baby." I walked out of that appointment with my head held high and a smile on my face as I looked at Ray. I have never viewed myself as a "lemon" since that day.

What is a Good-Enough Mom?

When I was a graduate student studying psychology, I came across an interesting theory of family therapy. It was called the "good-enough parent" by D.W. Winnicott. Winnicott developed this concept to provide support for families who he believed had "sound instincts" and were "stable and healthy families."[11] The theory stated that a parent did not have to be perfect in his/her role as a parent, but instead be "good enough." A successful parent needed to provide consistent love, warmth and security for their children, understanding that every parent would fail at times.

What is interesting and extremely applicable for us today is that Winnicott developed his theory to defend "ordinary" good mothers from two dangerous extremes that were coming from psychology. One extreme was the intrusion of professionalism on the ordinary family. This means that parents are in danger of being bombarded with professional expertise, so they doubt their own parenting abilities and instincts. The other extreme was idealization which emphasizes the nurturing environment that parents need to provide for their children. Winnicott feared that the family psychology movement would create the pressure of an idealized family that did not exist in reality. Winnicott's "good-enough parent" theory means that no mother can love her own kids perfectly or create the perfect nurturing environment. We all have character flaws that will negatively impact our parenting, but "good-enough parents," "good-enough moms" can be successful in raising kids to be healthy, functioning adults.

I think D.W. Winnicott was a modern-day prophet! Can you see the extremes he predicted all around us in our culture? Professionalization and idealization (what I would call perfectionism) scream at us as moms, don't they? We are not moms for very long before we are told how important it is to "listen to the experts," and we continually have ideals pushed on us of what we are "supposed to be doing" as a parent. A recent visit to the town library is a great example of another "ideal" that assaulted me out of the blue. I kept noticing a sign in the children's section that read, "1,000 Books Before Kindergarten." Yes, these signs were suggesting that kids should have read 1,000—not 100—books *before* kindergarten. Fantastic! A simple trip to the library (which is a good thing for a mom to do, right?) led to another new ideal I was not reaching. *The world of moms!*

Professionalization and perfectionism have led many moms down a road full of doubt, guilt, and deceit. These three enemies have the ability to continually drain us of our "Mom Joy" if we let them.

Doubt is that dubious emotion that makes us mistrust our own God-given mom instincts and forget our own strengths. As moms, we know our kids better than anyone else does, especially if we have been committed to a heart-connected relationship with them. There is a verse in James that gives us a great visual picture of doubt: *For the one who doubts is like a wave of the sea that is driven and tossed by the wind."—James 1:6b*

Have you felt like that, tossed about by the wind? And if we can feel like that, don't you think your kids can have similar feelings when we doubt ourselves as mothers? Doubting our mom instincts also leads to forgetting our strengths. I want to encourage you to parent from your strengths, not your weaknesses! Remember the baseball mom who asked me to name my strengths? Well now I know I have many strengths. Some of my strengths as a mom are flexibility, fun, and creativity. I would rather take my kids to a thousand places before I read them a thousand books. Not to say that I do not like reading, but I really like *going*. And that is not only good, it is spectacular. When I can parent by focusing on my strengths, rather than my weaknesses, I am being more than a "good-enough mom."

Some of the best advice I got as a mom was to structure the time I had with my kids around my interests and abilities. While I have not read 1,000 books to my children before kindergarten, I do enjoy reading to my kids—especially history. So, my kids got a lot of history read to them. Because it interests me, I am able to make it interesting to the kids. When I started following this advice in my homeschool, the days became more fun for everyone, because I was having fun. I had to embrace that I could not do it all. I gave myself permission to let my time with my kids revolve around the subjects that I enjoyed the most because this made our home happier and encouraged a love of learning.

Happiness and joy in our homes—in contrast with stress and anxiety—will intrinsically help our kids pursue their own strengths and interests. While I like history, my son JD is not a history enthusiast. While we did not share a love of history, somehow, he did pick up a love of learning. He was only eight years old when he would get the Kingfisher Science Encyclopedia and take it to his bed to study electricity. His room—to the chagrin of his older brother—was like a junk yard of abandoned appliances and electronic devices because he had a fascination with taking everything apart. It was about this time in his life that JD decided he wanted to be an engineer, and he has never wavered in that pursuit. So even though I am bored to death by science and would rather teach history all day, JD found his passion in science. I did not have to provide my kids with the perfect homeschool, but the "good-enough" homeschool, and I did it by schooling according to *my strengths*.

Another enemy we battle frequently as moms is guilt. In order to understand guilt better, I looked it up in the 1828 Webster dictionary. I find this dictionary so helpful because it shows me how far we have fallen as a society in our use and comprehension of the English language. The definition of guilt is quite interesting.

Guilt, noun

Criminality; that state of a moral agent which results from his actual commission of a crime or offense, knowing it to be a crime, or violation of the law. To constitute *guilt* there must be a moral agent enjoying freedom of will, and capable of distinguishing between right and wrong, and a willful or intentional violation of a known law, or rule of duty.

You might notice first that guilt is not a feeling, but instead a state of being. How often I have said to myself and to others *I feel guilty*. In fact, guilt is my personal ultimate nemesis. There have been days that guilt was piggy-backing my every move. Again, that spirit of perfectionism was the culprit. It is impossible to see all the things you are doing well when the voice of guilt lingers continually in your head. Your guilty thoughts often turn into guilty words, and then you are literally guilting yourself into misery. Romans 8:1 was a verse I knew, but was far from living out in my life: *Therefore there is now no condemnation for those who are in Christ Jesus.* As a Christian, my state of being is "not guilty" because God has declared me "not guilty" regardless of my feelings.

While this verse speaks specifically to Christians, which I will explain more in a future chapter, it important to distinguish between feelings of guilt and the state of guilt. Even though I believed Romans 8:1, I was not believing the truth. Feelings of guilt about falling short of idealistic standards were causing me much distress. By putting to death the spirit of perfectionism, I began to listen to the voice of the Holy Spirit telling me, "I am pleased with you." When I started listening to that voice, above the lies of guilt, it was like a fresh breeze blowing through my soul. God is pleased with me....sigh and rest.

Many times, I have been in conversations with weary moms as they pour out to me their concerns over all their burdens for their kids. When I tell them that God is pleased with them, tears immediately fill their eyes. Having this experience over and over with moms all over the country has shown me how many moms need to hear this message. Let me say it loud and clear, if you love your kids enough that you are reading a book about being a good mom, **God is pleased with you.**

I may someday write a whole book about guilt, but this is not that book. What I am not saying is that we should never feel convicted or sorry for things we do wrong. If we can't say, "I was wrong" to our kids, we have a parenting problem. We will explore this further in the third part of the book. But conviction and condemnation are two different things. Conviction is rooted in truth and a calling upward to do things differently. Guilt is rooted in lies and a downward pressure toward misery and failure. Remember, the road of professionalization and perfectionism leads to doubt, guilt, and deceit.

Many of you have resonated deeply with this chapter. In the midst of motherhood, you have been deceived into either thinking you have no great strengths or that your weaknesses overpower your strengths. Your weaknesses seem to be staring at you every day and no one is giving you a job review that is highlighting your strengths. Guess what? You have to give yourself the review! It is time to take a full accounting of all your strengths, gifts, abilities and even resources. It is time to celebrate all that you are doing right, all that is going well, and all the blessings you have. It is time to laser-focus on all that is good about you! You are far more than "good-enough." Kill perfectionism before it completely kills your joy! You are never going to have perfect character, the perfect home, or perfect kids, so don't wait to celebrate the really good. *Celebrate now.*

At the end of this chapter, I have given you another Mom Mission. May I encourage you to take immediate action on this one? Find a piece of paper and write down all your strengths. I am suggesting this also to encourage myself because it is a good exercise for us all. I am committed to writing down all my strengths, abilities, special gifts and resources. Even ask your spouse, close friends and co-workers to contribute their thoughts. You can ask your kids; just make sure they know they can only say strengths because, as you know, kids have a great way of regularly pointing out our weaknesses, right? But we are going to be determined to know and be thankful for our many, many strengths. By doing this, we are going to release more gratitude and joy in our own hearts and homes. Celebrate all that is good about you.

Mom Mission #7

Know your strengths.

Chapter 8
Great-Enough Kids

Most moms think their kids are above and beyond extraordinary from the day they are born. At least that is what I think about my kids. Of course, I do not go around saying this to other people, but I am glad to think this way. It is a blessing. We want to champion our kids because our kids are great. God wants you to believe your kids are wonderful, fantastic, extraordinary and unique because guess what—that is how God thinks about you.

It is only normal that we want the whole world to see what we see. However, as our kids get older and fall short of the expectations we have—whether it be in behavior, intelligence, skills, or appearances—we can let our standards smother our kids. I think we moms have that beautiful picture in our mind's eye of all the wonderful things our kids can do, all the beauty they can bring to the world, all the possibilities.

Potential is a wonderful thing. It is full of hope and expectation. However, expectation can be both good and bad. When expectation becomes idealistic standards, then it is not so good. Having idealistic standards (or we might call it that pesky perfectionistic spirit) can be one of the most fool-proof ways of shutting down heart-connected relationships with our kids because *no one* likes standards that seem impossible to attain. When our kids are under this perfectionistic pressure from us, guess what they do? They close their hearts.

Most kids—dare I say all—do not like disappointing Mom. In fact, Mom's disappointment is often more than they can bear. It is easy to get blind-sided into thinking our goal in raising children is for them to achieve success in all the areas in which they are amazingly gifted. It makes sense, right? You know the image we have pictured in our perfect vision for each of our wonderful children? We *know* how great they are. Isn't it always a good thing that we help them reach their full potential?

Actually, the answer is no. It is not a good thing to hold our idealistic standards for our kids' potential *if* it starts to eat away at the relationship that we want to have with them. Remember the goal—lifelong, heart-connected discipleship relationships. Moms, our main mission is making sure we keep the primary goal, the *primary* goal. So, my question to you in this chapter is, are *you* okay with having *great-enough kids?*

What are Great-Enough Kids?

I hope you do think you have great kids. Moms should be champions of their kids. They should be their best cheerleaders, encouragers, and most of all—believe in them. As a Mom, I often believe in my kids far more than they believe in themselves. My goal is that while they are in our home, they are being nurtured and inspired in such a way that when they launch into the not-so-nurturing environments in this world, they will carry my view of them within their own hearts.

Most of us believe we have great kids, but none of us think our kids are great *all the time!* There are those days when we are desperate for the babysitter to come. As they get older, even into adulthood, we go through difficult seasons with feelings of frustration with our kids. But in general, most moms believe they have great kids.

Back to that same baseball game—you know when I realized I had been so obsessed with my faults that it blinded me to my strengths? On that long drive home, I also wondered how my perfectionism lenses had shaded my perspective about my kids. Had I also been blinded to their strengths? The answer was no. It was not difficult to mentally list all of the great things about each of my kids. However, there were two big problems with my perspective that began to come clear as I was driving. Just like I was hyper-focused on all of my faults, I had that same similar hyper-focus when it came to my kids' character traits and giftedness. While I believed my kids were great,

I started to wonder if I was subtly pushing them to ask themselves, "Am I great-enough for Mom?"

That pesky spirit of perfectionism had a way of directing my attention to the things that I needed to fix in my kids. And my general mindset with all things that need fixing is that it needs to happen yesterday. That list I had for myself—you know the one that is both exhaustive and endless—I had those lists for my kids, too. The lists were noble—very noble! I mentally listed things that needed to be fixed in their characters, life-skills, study habits, athletic pursuits, and social circles. Problems with their relationships with each other and problems with the way they treated their things. Lots of issues needed to be fixed! Lots of problems needed to be solved! Lots of opportunities that should not be missed!

Let me tell you how this might play out in our home. Let's say I am walking in the house after I have been out, and I have left the job of cleaning the kitchen to the kids. The first thing my eyes see is the small pile of dirty dishes left in the sink—even though the rest of the kitchen is relatively clean. What do you think are the first words out of my mouth? Are they, "Thank you for cleaning the kitchen," or "Why did you leave dirty dishes in the sink?" If you guessed the latter, you would be correct. My mind goes aimlessly to the detail that was wrong, and out of my mouth I pronounce my disappointment without even thinking. As opposed to saying thank you and praising what was done right and then maybe gently asking, "Why are there still dishes in the sink?"

On the drive home from that same baseball game, I asked myself, *how frequently am I noticing and acknowledging all the good things happening in my kids and in my home? Am I smothering my kids with perfectionism just like I had been smothering myself?* My kids may be wondering, *"Will we ever be great-enough?"*

Just one example of something I was stressing about on that drive home was whether we were making the right choice about my son's baseball team. Was it maximizing his opportunities? Did we miss the chance for him to play D1 baseball? He is a great player, but is he great-enough? Even while I was internally processing these thoughts, the Holy Spirit broke through. RW was very happy. He was happy to be on this trip. He was thanking me for coming with him, as opposed to sending him with another family because it was always hard for me to get away with so many demands at home. RW knew this was a sacrifice of time and that other kids were going to be missing me. Here I was in the middle of a mother-son trip with RW, an experience that was rare for sure! He was sharing with me his dreams, his concerns and his heart, AND he was asking me about my life as well. RW was really enjoying his time with me. RW was not stressing about being "great-enough" at all.

Remember when I asked my daughter Lissy if she knew I was proud of her and she said, "No"? I wish I could say that I completely changed the lenses of my mommy glasses that day, but I have learned changing those perfectionist lenses takes a long time, many trials, many mom mistakes, many tears, and many lessons of learning and re-learning. I am thankful that God does not give up on me. He does not give up on you either. It is a constant mental shift for me to continue to keep the focus of my mothering on life-long, heart-connected relationships because it is so counter-cultural.

Does any mom ever ask you how your relationship is going with your kids? No, most of our mom conversations are focused on what are kids are doing and the problems they are facing or the problems we are having with them. Mom conversations tend to revolve around problems. Personally, I would like to change that. The truth is our kids may be achieving success in a lot of areas of their lives but we moms are still problem focused. Is it any wonder that this can lead to relational hurt? While our kids can have a lot of great things happening in their lives, they may at the same time be disconnected from a heart-connected relationship with us. Don't you want to be a part of it all? I know I do.

If we want to continue having a voice of influence, encouragement, and help in our kids' lives then we should pay attention to the relational red flags—not just our kids' achievements. Maybe our mom conversations should be about how our relationships with our kids are doing. "Do your kids share their hearts with you?" "What are you doing in your home to build heart-connection with your kids?"

Standing up to the Mom-Push

Take a minute and look closely at the world our kids are growing up in today. While many of the ideas in this book can apply to different cultures around the world, the idea of "great-enough" kids is especially relevant to American culture. While I cannot say for sure when it started, I can say for as long as I have been a mother, I have felt what I refer to as a "constant push." The "push" that moms experience even from the time our kids are babies is a push to *do* more and *expect* more from our kids. This sense that we as moms need to make sure we are maximizing our kids' fullest potential in every area is frankly overwhelming. Every area of our kids' development—social, physical, athletic, intellectual, emotional and spiritual—all seem to demand a "push."

I do not want to say there are not times when we need to push our children. Our nine-year-old Ray went on a trip last summer with his grandparents and his cousin. While he was excited to go, he was also quite anxious about the whole thing. There were several "mom-pushes" that were needed to help Ray overcome his fear and enjoy the trip. It is not that we never need to push our kids, but we need to do it according to our decision about what is best for our kids—not pressure from the culture around us.

This pressure applies to all moms, whether they are at home with their kids or in the workforce. Somehow, we unconsciously believe the same lie—that we carry the responsibility to *raise our kids perfectly*. I realize that sounds ridiculous! Who actually believes that? Sadly, many of us do without realizing it. There is an underlying pressure we feel as moms to get it all right. We understand there is this little window of time called childhood, and we want to give our kids the best chance of success. We want them to be in great schools, great activities, and excel in it all. The cultural "mom-push" that I am referring to is that uneasy sensation that you can always be doing more for your kids. It is an idealistic expectation that you can pave a beautiful, smooth road for your kids which will enable them to drive right into the world of adult success.

Being blessed with many dear and wise friends who have kids slightly older than my oldest child, I have often clung to their wisdom. One of the best ways to learn as a mom is to regularly hang out with other moms who are in the next stage of parenting. If you have a teachable and humble spirit, it helps you become a better mom. One such "next stage" friend of mine, Stephanie, gave me this wisdom when my oldest son graduated from high school.

RW's high school experience had both ups and downs like most kids. His senior year was rather emotional for me. While much of it was filled with enjoying the fruit of all the hard work of parenting, there was for me a regular evaluation of my "mom choices." I was unprepared for the sense of regret I began to feel in questioning some of the choices Rob and I had made together. Did we make the right educational choices for him? Should I have pushed him to do percussion team? Would it have been better if I had sent him to the public school? These questions were not nearly as bad as the "should have" thoughts that regularly floated through my brain. Thoughts like, I should have pushed him to develop his math gifts more. I should have gone to more of his games. I should not have over-parented him so much. I was hard on myself unnecessarily because of that uneasy feeling that it was possible to parent without regrets, to parent perfectly.

My friend, Stephanie, gave me a beautiful picture that now guides me in my Mom Mission. She said, "Amy, when you look back at the 18 years of RW in your home, you are seeing a road with potholes and you are focusing on the potholes. What you are not seeing is the beautiful road. What is worse is that you actually think the road is supposed to have no potholes! There is no such thing as a smooth, paved road for any of our kids. Now let me tell you what you cannot see. As RW now leaves your home, you are going to see how God paves the potholes. God is going to fill—according to His plan, not yours, the potholes in RW's road."

You cannot parent without potholes. Whether the potholes are your mistakes, circumstances that you cannot change, a difficult school environment, or a lack of good friends, the path to adulthood will have potholes. They are unavoidable. Your kids and you will experience many disappointments in the growing-up years. By the time our kids are 18, some of their childhood dreams will have come and gone. They may never play on the varsity basketball team, never make a school musical, never have a close group of friends, and never get asked to a high school dance. If we are honest with ourselves, we will admit that these dreams were not just for our kids; they were our dreams as well.

When dreams aren't coming true, where do you want your kids to go for comfort and guidance? I want them to come to me or their dad. If my kids feel that my most important goal was pushing them to greatness, then I know they will not come to me when greatness is eluding them. However, if heart-connected relationship is clearly the most important goal in parenting, then my kids will want to come to me when their dreams are fading. They will not value themselves based on their performance. Instead my kids will *know* they are valued by me for who they are.

Mom, you can't do it all and your kids can't do it all. Stand up to the "Mom-Push" and start pushing back. In part three, I will share with you some of the counter-cultural ways that helped me prioritize heart-connected relationships above all the pressures that moms face daily. You may not believe it, but your kids do want to have heart-connected relationships with you. A loving relationship with you builds resilience in your kids to deal with the inevitable disappointments that are part of life—everyone's life. Make sure your kids know today that you are pleased with them for who they are rather than what they are becoming. Let them know they are great-enough!

Mom Mission #8

Make sure your kids know they are great-enough for you.

Chapter 9
What Does God Want from You?

Day by day, day by day
Oh, dear Lord, three things I pray
To see Thee more clearly
Love Thee more dearly
Follow Thee more nearly
Day by day

Andrew Lloyd Weber, GodSpell

What dreams did you have when you were a kid? That is an easy question for me. I dreamed of being a singer, a dancer, and a writer—but most of all I dreamed of being a mom. From playing with baby dolls to babysitting, I knew I wanted to be a mom. In fact, the dream of being a mom superseded my other dreams. Every pursuit that I considered undertaking was followed by this question, "How will this life work with being a mom?"

Like many women of my generation, I was taught that I could do it all. I could have a great career and satisfying motherhood. The message was to prepare for career, then motherhood would be the easy part. That is why I was far more prepared for my career than motherhood. You will notice that "marriage and family therapist" was not on my dream list as a kid, but it seemed at the time the best pursuit to fit with my mom dream. While I both danced and sang in college, I did not see a path to follow those dreams that would fit well into motherhood and family. I did not want to wait to start a family. It was my dream.

I know it was my mom who gave me the heart and passion for motherhood. While she worked as a math teacher, community coordinator and earned a masters degree in mathematics, she also made it crystal clear that her favorite role was being Mom. I obviously saw something in her that I knew I wanted. Any desire for career was overshadowed by my stronger desire to not miss the best thing, to not miss being a mom. And let me take a moment to say this clearly, if we have the blessing of being a mom then let us remember that it is a privilege and a gift. Not every little girl who dreams of being a mom gets to be one. It is a title we cannot ever take for granted.

It did not take long for me to realize that motherhood was not the easy part of my life, and my years of college and graduate school had not quite prepared me for this Mom Mission. I have already chronicled for you the guilt and feelings of failure that often plagued me as a mother. It is hard to be in the middle of motherhood wishing you had been more prepared for the task. The only training you get is on-the-job training. Is it any wonder that moms can see their failures more than their strengths? Each day, as our kids are getting older and entering into new phases of development, we are making new mistakes. You cannot master a phase because when you think you have perfected something, everything changes again!

Motherhood changed me. One of the things that changed first was my faith. Because being a mom had always been my dream, I wanted to do it right. I wanted to be a great mom most of all.

In Matthew 9:36, we read about Jesus' attitude toward those who are lost and struggling. *When he saw the crowds, he had compassion for them, because they were harassed and helpless, like sheep without a shepherd.* This verse reminded me that Jesus was full of compassion toward me. He was not constantly disappointed that I was falling short; He wanted to help me. He wanted to gently lead me. I was greatly encouraged. God has compassion on His children—all of his children.

While I had been reading the Bible my whole life, I had not read it through the lens of being a parent. The Bible is "living and active" (Hebrews 4:12). This is why we can never over-study God's Word.

Sometime after I had four children, I began to read the Bible as the ultimate parenting manual. If I wanted to be the best mom I could be, I needed to start with the perfect role model in Scripture. I could study and understand how God is a Father to me and seek to follow His example as I parented my children. God wants a heart-connected, life-long discipleship relationship with me! God desires for me to stay connected with Him—to abide with Him. The more I remain in Him, the more He will help me do all the good works He has planned for me to do, and being a good mom is certainly a good work. Relationship is what God wants most with His children.

God desires to reconcile us to Himself.

All this is from God, who through Christ reconciled us to himself and gave us the ministry of reconciliation; that is, in Christ God was reconciling the world to himself, not counting their trespasses against them, and entrusting to us the message of reconciliation. –2 Corinthians 5:18-19.

What does reconcile mean? It means God wants to restore relationship with His children. He made us acceptable to Him. He *made us acceptable moms.* God accepts us in our current state, and by sending His Son to die for all of our sins—including our mistakes, character flaws and failures—He gives us the perfection of Jesus. Our heavenly Father does not demand perfection from us, instead He gives us His perfection. When we repent of our sins and believe in the name of Jesus Christ, we receive the righteousness we so desperately desire. God accepts us in Christ. God is pleased with us.

Read that again, God is pleased with you. God accepts you. God wants a heart-connected, life-long, discipleship relationship with you because He loves you. Does this sound familiar? God is not trying to get you to some standard of character and then disconnect from you so you can go off and do great things. His primary goal is for you to abide with Him every day, day by day. He wants you to know Him just as He knows you. Jesus tells us that this is the most important commandment in the Bible: *You shall love the Lord your God with all your heart and with all your soul and with all your might. And these words that I command you today shall be on your heart. –Deuteronomy 6:5-6.* God wants our hearts, not our efforts to make ourselves perfect.

God desires to discipline us just as any loving father disciplines his children. Don't you discipline your kids because you love them, not because you hate them? His discipline in our lives will lead us to repentance and obedience—not an overflowing fountain of guilt. Repentance is a key part of that gentle leading. We need to understand true repentance, which is actually a beautiful gift from God. It is when He allows us to see the sin in our life, the ways we miss the mark of His perfection, and the errors in our thinking and behavior. He then blesses us with a desire to turn toward Him, trust Him with our lives, and learn to walk in His ways. True repentance leads us to feel closer to God and full of hope—not despair.

Daily focusing on my relationship with God is not something that comes easy for me. For some reason, I find myself always looking for the right "system." I have a tendency to falsely believe that if I can just find the right "plan," the "right discipline," the right "way" to run my life then all of a sudden everything will just "click." But Jesus says, *I am the way, the truth, and the life* (John 14:6). **Jesus is the Way.** Jesus is the "system" I was always searching to find. Day by day, I desire to see Him more, love Him more and follow Him more. The truth is that there is no "system" that can ever replace a daily relationship with Jesus.

Jesus said to him, 'I am the way, and the truth, and the life. No one comes to the Father except through me' (John 14:6). When your relationship has been made right with God through Jesus, you are then a member of His family. From this position, you can be sure that feelings of "guilt" are not coming from God. Most people are familiar with the verse John 3:16, *For God so loved the world that He gave his only son, that whoever believes in Him should not perish, but have eternal life.* Then keep reading on in verses 17-18, *For God did not send the Son into the world to condemn the world, but in order that the world might be saved through him. Whoever believes in him is not condemned, but whoever does not believe is condemned already, because he has not believed in the name of the only Son of God.*

God desires to shepherd us—not condemn us. Shepherding comes from a heart of love while condemnation is the state of being declared guilty for your sins. If you trust in Jesus Christ as your Savior, you are not condemned for your sins, but instead your sins are paid for by the sacrifice of Jesus' death on the cross. Your condemnation was put on Christ! Therefore, feelings of guilt are not the way our Shepherd leads us, so we have to reject those feelings and receive God's lovingkindness toward us. Consider Romans 2:4, as it is written in the Amplified Version,

> Or do you have no regard for the wealth of His kindness and tolerance and patience [in withholding His wrath]? Are you [actually] unaware or ignorant [of the fact] that God's kindness leads you to repentance [that is, to change your inner self, your old way of thinking—seek His purpose for your life]? (AMP)

This to me is one of the most beautiful phrases in Scripture, *His kindness leads to our repentance.*

This is the foundation of the discipleship relationship that God wants to have with us. He gently leads His children. We grow through seeking Him, reading His Word, and responding in repentance and obedience. True repentance always makes us feel closer to God and good about ourselves because we know how much God loves us. In contrast, guilt will fill us with negative feelings about ourselves and drive us away from God into deeper self-focus. Have you noticed that? Guilt has a way of making us more consumed with ourselves so that we can even justify self-pity parties. I also see this manifest itself in my kids. Frequently, I have to gently disciple my kids about the difference between true repentance and feelings of guilt. Overflowing guilt is not life-giving for us or our kids. Jesus came that we may have life, and have it to the full (John 10:10).

God desires a relationship with me —not just for my own benefit—but so He can make an appeal through me to others. *Therefore, we are ambassadors for Christ, God making his appeal through us. We implore you on behalf of Christ, be reconciled to God* (2 Corinthians 5:20). Can you see how this all flows together? This ministry begins with our children. We can show kindness to them and pray for them to be reconciled to God. This is because God wants a relationship with my kids more than He wants them to display great behavior, character, athletic skills, musical gifts, etc. God wants a heart-connected, life-long, discipleship relationship with them. It is an absolutely beautiful vision, isn't it?

One of our mottos in Visionary Parenting—the parenting ministry that Rob and I have together—is that the world does not need more beautiful children, smart children, athletic children, popular children, or musical children...the world needs more godly children. These are children that have a heart-connected, life-long, discipleship relationship with Jesus Christ, day by day. They will make lots of mistakes, have big problems, character flaws, and personal failures, but they will know God and love Him because they belong to Him. They will have a personal relationship with Him. Moms, we are Christ's ambassadors to our own kids—as if God is making His appeal through us for our kids to be reconciled and restored in their relationships with Him. We can do this; God is cheering for us all the way.

Why do we all desire perfection? We were created for it. God wants to have loving relationship with all the children He created. For God so loved *the world,* which includes you and your kids. He desires to give His children the perfection we crave—not only for eternity in heaven—but to begin His blessings here and now. When we trust Him with our lives, He sees us as righteous, pleasing, and acceptable, because He sees us through Jesus. God is pleased with His children. Moms, **God is pleased with you!** He wants all of us to desire a relationship with Him characterized by loving Him, honoring Him, and listening to Him. God wants to have a heart-connected, life-long, discipleship relationship with you. Jesus lived a perfect life and died on the cross so that we might be completely forgiven of our sins and made righteous before God. This desire we have for all the wrongs to be made right is a good desire, and God has made it possible through His Son Jesus.

God Desires Day by Day Connection

Last Mother's Day, I had some time alone on Sunday afternoon. I decided to treat myself by going into one of my favorite clothing stores to browse the sales rack. I found a few nice items, so I went to the sales desk to purchase them where I found myself overhearing the middle of a conversation.

> The sales clerk seemed to know the woman who was checking out in front of me. The clerk asked her, "Have they called yet?"
>
> The woman sighed sadly, "No, not yet. That is why I am out shopping for myself." I could tell this woman's love bucket was not getting filled by the items she was purchasing.
>
> The clerk answered, "There is still a lot of day left. Maybe they will call later."
>
> "Maybe," the woman answered, with little hope, as she walked out of the store.

As I walked around the outdoor mall on that Mother's Day afternoon, I reflected on that overheard conversation. It made me sad. Do I want to raise kids that obey my standards, live according to their "full potential," and then disappear out of my life? Would that make *me* happy? No, I desire for my kids to love me back. I will not require or need daily contact with my kids as they grow older, but I want to still be connected. I certainly will want my kids to call me on Mother's Day, not from obligation, but because they *love me*. I do want the love and care that I have poured into my children to be reciprocated. And guess what? Your heavenly Father wants that, too. You are still His child. He wants to have a relationship with *you* day by day.

Can you see it now? Can you see how this "perfectly" models what God wants with us? He wants to have a loving relationship with you. God does not just want you to obey all His rules, live to your full potential, and walk away from Him. He does not need you to find the perfect "way" to be a Mom because He is the way. No, God wants His children to desire a relationship with Him just like you want your children to desire a relationship with you.

God sent Jesus to the world so that He could have a relationship with His children, which is what He has always wanted. As Moms, I think we understand this well. While we set standards and rules that we want our children to obey, our goal is not to raise robots who perform certain tasks. *You cannot have relationships with robots.* This parenting priority on relationship mirrors God's priority on relationship. God's purpose for your life is not a robotic following of rules apart from a love relationship with Him. He wants our hearts, and when He has our hearts, we are eager to serve and obey Him. So, I am asking you now, do you desire a relationship with God day by day?

Mom Mission #9

Remember you are God's child and
He wants a daily relationship with you.

➤ *Part* 3 ⫸
Our Relationship Action Plan

We do not often put the words *relationship* and *action* in the same sentence. *Action* makes us think of pursuing tasks and *relationship* makes us think of pausing for people. In this section, I am giving you ideas for an "action plan" to help build heart-connected relationships with your kids.

This is not in any way an exhaustive list. I am simply sharing some of the ups and downs I have learned through my mothering experience that have helped me focus on building relationships with my kids. Remember, I still have several young ones in my home, so I continue experiencing successes and failures in my motherhood just like you do. However, I hope this section gives you some practical take-aways to help in whatever stage of motherhood you find yourself. This action plan is not perfect, and of course I do not follow it perfectly. If you skipped reading sections one and two for the sake of expediency, you missed the foundation you need to understand why this action plan is focused on relationship-building as opposed to discipline.

There is more to good parenting than just building heart-connected, life-long discipleship relationships. So, if you are reading this section and have a lot of unanswered questions about parenting, I encourage you to check out our book *Visionary Parenting*. My purpose is not to suggest a "feel-good/be best friends with your kids and everything will be awesome" approach. That is not the purpose of this relational action plan. Instead, here are some positive steps you can take toward building great relationships with your kids.

Chapter 10
Building Blocks

Good relationships do not just happen; good relationships require work. We build relationships. There are some basic ingredients that are essential: love and trust. Love means so many things, but let me try to make it as simple as I can. Love means that you want good for another person, not bad, and that you are not giving up on them, you are committed. Trust means that there is honesty, openness and security between people. We all want families characterized by love and trust. This does not mean everyone likes each other all the time. This does not mean that we don't have conflict. This does not mean we are not disappointed, hurt and angry with one another at times, maybe a lot more times than we would prefer. However, it does mean we continue loving and trusting each other even through all the bad feelings. Feelings will come and go but love and trust needs to remain.

We cannot love perfectly or trust each other perfectly. In our family, I can trust my husband with the big, important things in our lives. Yet in the day to day running of our home, we can have communication, personality and character problems that can lead to distrust. For example, I tend to run late to almost everything. So, when I tell my husband Rob that I am going to be on time to an important event, he understandably has a hard time "trusting" that I am actually going to be punctual. His experiences with me would say that I am probably not going to be on time, but he knows I am going to be there. So, while he distrusts that I will make it on time, he trusts that I am doing my best to stick to my word. This is imperfect trust.

We also regularly experience imperfect love. As a mom you are aware of the moments that you lose your temper and hear something come out of your mouth that you know you will regret and will need to apologize for. We can say some pretty awful things to our kids and loved ones, but still love them with all our hearts. This is part of real life and real relationships. Yet love is demonstrated because we do not give up and we keep wanting and pursuing the best for our families, regardless of the hard times.

Therefore, love and trust are the core foundations for all good relationships. What can we do to build relationships that are filled with love and trust? This chapter is a short list of some of the important principles that have helped me build heart-connected relationships with my kids. This list was created with years of lots of trials and lots of errors, but lots and lots of heart-warming success. My hope is that this list gives you some ideas for building heart-connected relationships with your own kids, filled with imperfect love and imperfect trust, but perfectly real.

1. Affection, Affection, Affection

This should remind you of attachment, attachment, attachment! Affection is the pathway to attachment. I once heard a great "mom speaker" (for lack of a better title) say that you can never spoil a baby with too much affection. I would add that it is difficult to spoil any of our kids, regardless of their age, with too much affection. Spoiling means that you give something in excess that has a detrimental effect on the person's character. We can spoil them with too many things, too much freedom, too many sweets and a host of other things, but can we spoil our kids with too much affection? I don't think so. I have ended most nights cuddling my younger kids while tucking them into bed, and then waking them up to morning snuggles. Being raised in a home with lots of physical affection, even my older teenage boys still feel comfortable giving and receiving lots of hugs. Physical affection builds heart connection in younger and older kids.

However, affection does not have to exclusively be physical affection. A double bacon cheeseburger after a baseball game shows affection toward my teenage boys probably more than a hug would, and the right Starbucks® drink at the right time delivers the same kind of affectionate message to my girls.

Affection has a lot to do with looking at your kid's life, at whatever stage they are in, and trying to communicate your love in a tangible way. Even if you have adult kids out of your home, you can ask God to show you how to communicate affection to them. The Webster's Dictionary® definition of affection uses this phrase: "A permanent bent of the mind, formed by the presence of an object, or by some act of another person, and existing without the presence of its object."[13] I know that is crazy wordy, but I love that visual picture of affection—our mind is permanently bent toward our kids. It does not matter whether our kids are close or far, there is part of our minds that is fixed on their well-being. Affection helps form the foundation of our attachment with our children, but it can also rebuild relationships that have broken.

Affection in the midst of conflict is powerful. My daughter Laynie is entering the high school years and we tend to have more daily conflict than in previous years. A common cause of conflict is clothing. Whether it is about borrowing clothes, taking proper care of clothes, or agreeing on the types of clothes to wear, we can have several negative interactions each week that take a toll on our relationship. Recently I have decided to show affection to Laynie by saying, "Yes" when she asks to borrow my clothing. Even though we might have had conflict all week about clothing, I want to communicate affection to her at this stage of life. When I let her borrow something of value to me—despite her imperfect track record of taking good care of other people's things—I am communicating affection to her. The affection lets her know that I value our relationship even in the midst of conflict. I would encourage you to find out what communicates affection to your child(ren) and pursue it.

2. Teach Your Children to Honor You

Honor is an essential ingredient in building heart-connected discipleship relationships with your kids. Remember that the mother-child relationship is special. When your kids are self-sufficient adults, they will not be required to obey you. We do not want to have children we are trying to control, but we do want to have kids that have been raised to honor us. Does that sound selfish? It shouldn't.

I assume you are training your children to respect their teachers. If your kids play a sport, I am confident that you are encouraging them to listen and follow the coach's direction. Respect, listening, and obeying are components of honoring relationships. You are continually teaching your kids to honor the people in authority over them, but if you do not teach your own kids to honor you, no one else is going to do it. Numerous times in the Bible we read instructions about honoring and obeying our parents. Honor for parents ought to be above honor for teachers and coaches. But kids have to be taught and trained to honor their parents, because it does not just happen.

We have to use this word "honor" in our home early and often. I have found that age three is an important window for training my children about honor. For example, if a child is having a temper outburst because of not getting her own way, after dealing with the behavior you can teach her about honor. I explain to the child that it is not honoring to Mom to act that way when I do not give her what she wants. I am not shaming her, I am training her in a positive and loving way, explaining what honor is. This is just the beginning of the training, introducing the concept of honor into the child's vocabulary. Developing a culture of honor in the home with each of our children will require ongoing training.

Honor is not a lesson that any of us can learn all at once. As a married woman with children, I am still learning what it means to honor my parents as they get older. In fact, there was a season in my life that my prayer partner, Stephanie, and I would regularly ask the Lord to give us a heart of greater honor toward our parents. We were encouraging each other through the hurts that we carried from our parents (and all of us have hurts from our parents), to not only forgive completely, but also raise our parents up in honor as the Bible commands in the fifth commandment: *Honor your father and mother, so that your days may be prolonged in the land the Lord your God gives you* (Exodus 20:12 AMP). Stephanie and I knew that we needed the Lord to give us hearts of honor toward our own parents if we wanted to be successful in training our children to honor us. In order to have heart-connected, life-long, discipleship relationships with our kids, we need to strive to create a culture of honor in our homes and in our own hearts.

3. Learn to say, "I am sorry" and, "I was wrong"

We have all made mistakes, are making mistakes, and will make more mistakes. When we mess up, we have to own it— in front of our kids. For example, maybe I speak to my kids in a sarcastic and shaming way because I am frustrated with a bad behavior. If I feel bad about how I spoke to them but never say, "I am sorry, that was wrong of me to speak to you like that," then I am not taking ownership of my behavior.

I think it is common to feel bad about our mistakes, but I think it is uncommon for us to directly own our mistakes. When a lot of our time is spent dealing with our kids' bad behavior, it is easy to give ourselves a pass. We say something like, "Well, I would not have yelled at you if you did not lose your backpack again." I realize it is hard to say, "I am sorry for yelling" while your kids are repeating over and over the same frustrating behaviors. Is it too contrite to admit two wrongs do not make a right? The truth is, someone has to be the adult and lead by saying, "I am sorry for losing my temper and that is wrong."

If you look closely at our culture today, we have a large number of people who really do think that their bad behavior is justified by someone else's bad behavior. Would you like to see culture change in this area? Let it start in your home. Let it start with you. When you hurt your kids—intentionally or unintentionally—say, "I am sorry." When you are wrong about something, say, "I was wrong." You cannot overestimate how this will help your kids do the same thing as they grow up. I promise that eventually you will hear them say back to you, "Mom, I am sorry," and "Mom, I was wrong." Be patient with the process.

4. Be a Teachable Expert

Have you ever met the new mom who already seems to have all the answers? I am confident that I came across that way sometimes as a new mom (I hope not too much, but it does make me cringe when I think of it). I will always have blind spots about myself and about my kids. Having a teachable spirit is essential as a mom because our kids perceive that we are willing to learn, grow, and change just like we are guiding them in the same process. A teachable mom will raise teachable kids.

In order to stand up to the "Mom-Push" I mentioned earlier, we have to act on our expertise about our own kids. My daughter Lissy had a lot of social anxiety when she was a child. One situation that was difficult for her was attending birthday parties. At ages five through seven (maybe even later), Lissy could not attend her friends' birthday parties without me. She would rather not go to the party if it meant being anxious during the event. I had *lots* of people telling me how I should handle her issues. I received some condescending, snarky comments from other moms when I attended the birthday parties of Lissy's friends. The bottom line was that I had to trust my own instincts as to the best way to handle Lissy's anxiety despite the other expert opinions. I prayed a lot and listened to the voice of the Holy Spirit. I knew Lissy the best, and I believed this was the best way to help her. This journey became something that connected our hearts as we got through it together. If you met her today, you would have a hard time believing that she was an anxious little girl for many years.

Can I encourage you to be the teachable expert for each of your kids?

5. Accept Yourself

Did you know that you can grow more through your strengths than you can in your weaknesses? How is that for life changing? Accept yourself as a mom and do the things you enjoy with your kids, remembering that you do not have to excel at it all. Of course, we should also be willing to do things that are out of our comfort zone when our kids want us to participate. I realize we have to spend more time in the areas of our strengths or else life gets exhausting. If I tried to do crafts with my kids all the time, I would not be a very happy mom. Crafts are an area of relative weakness for me, not strength. By growing more and more in my strengths, I am a lot happier. Happy moms create a lot more heart-connection with their kids.

When we are willing to enter the worlds of our children, they will love to have our attention and interest. Build a lot of your *relationship* with them around the things that you enjoy, especially when they are little. Enjoy these things together. This does not mean doing exclusively what you like to do and distracting your kids so you can enjoy your life. For example, if you like to shop and you are distracting your children with an iPad, then this does not qualify as enjoying an activity together. However, if you include a fun time at the mall playground where you are engaged with your children, talking with them and engaging their interests during your mall trip, then you are having a fun shared experience for both you and your children. This is a better way to spend your time with them if crafts will leave you frustrated and your kids in tears. This is what I mean by parenting according to your strengths. Please do not hear that it is wrong to give your kids an iPad while you shop. Sometimes you have to get done what you need to get done or you simply need a break! I am suggesting that many of the activities you enjoy can be enjoyed *with* your kids. You do not need to completely reinvent yourself to be a good mom.

Learn to accept who you are in your role as mom. Find the things that both you and your kids can enjoy together and embrace those things that will bring a lot of joy in your home. For example, I don't enjoy growing a garden, but I enjoy being around people. I would rather take my kids to the pool instead of spend a lot of time growing vegetables. So, we ride our bikes to shop for our vegetables at the farmer's market and then have lots of fun together at the pool. Accepting myself helped me create more heart-connection experiences with my kids.

6. Accept Your Kids

The same truth applies to your kids as it does to you. Your children will be able to grow more in their strengths than they will in areas of weakness. Let me caution you though; in general, you will often not truly know your kids' strengths and weaknesses until they are in high school. Honestly, I would like to write a whole other book about the problem of attempting to identify a child's "giftedness" or "lack of giftedness" at a young age. Kids grow and change tremendously through the years, and their abilities do as well. If a seven-year-old is a good basketball player, it is way too soon to call him "a good athlete," and likewise it is way too soon to call a seven-year-old who is not a good basketball player a "bad athlete." When I hear the word "gifted" used to describe children, a red flag goes up in my thinking. It may be better to refer to what our young children *enjoy* as opposed to what they are *gifted* in.

I can remember sitting week after week in the women's locker room at Wheaton College with seven-year-old Laynie as she cried and refused to swim with the swim team. I had signed both JD and Laynie up for an eight-week session. They had practice twice each week and the college was close to our house so the commitment seemed fairly small. While they both were singled out as good swimmers, Laynie did not do many activities outside the home, and since she was so athletic I thought this was a good way for her to try something new. While the first practice was great, it went sour quickly. She became an expert at having headaches or stomachaches during every practice. Eventually, I was spending the whole practice time in the locker room with her in crying hysterics claiming she did not like it. Swimming was now causing significant relational stress for Laynie and me. While I was very frustrated with her lack of compliance, she was not only upset about swimming but also aware of how much she was disappointing me. After week four, I realized the best thing to do was to accept that while Laynie might be good at swimming, at this point she had a strong aversion to being "a swimmer." Accepting her hysterics about swimming even though I did not understand it, losing the money I had paid for the session, and pulling her out of the program ended up rescuing our relationship. I have no doubt that I made the right choice.

The *gift* you can give your child today is acceptance. Kids feel freer to take risks and try new things when they daily experience mom's acceptance and love. Our kids' strengths and weaknesses in areas of character and abilities will continue to fluctuate. Remember, they are valuable for who they are right now—not just who they are becoming. Communicate this to them with your actions and your words.

7. Consistently Care About the Important Things

Consistency in our parenting is daunting for a lot of us. We once tried to do an "If – Then" chart in our home. The goal of the chart was to have a clear plan of consequences for bad behavior. We also had a "Blessings Chart," which was a system of rewards for good behavior. I failed miserably at following these charts, but I am not failing as a mom! By the grace of God, I am raising great kids who are becoming compassionate and responsible adults, so I have done a lot of things right. Charts and systems do not determine success.

What do you care about the most? What would your kids say are the most important things to you? This is where consistency matters. If you consistently care about what is going on in your child's heart, then your kids will know that. You cannot hide what is most important to you from your kids; they can often see it more clearly than you can. If your child's academic success is the most important to you, your child will know it. If having a heart-connected life-long, discipleship relationship is important to you, then show that to your kids—consistently.

8. Secure and Flexible Boundaries

Boundaries give our children security. Security is another word for trust. You cannot have a solid relationship without trust. Moms have a huge responsibility for helping our kids learn trust. When a baby learns through experience that she will be taken care of, she is learning to trust. A visual picture for me is placing a baby in a Pack 'n Play®. We place them in a small, safe environment. As she grows older, her trust in us is also growing. We can expand her safe place from a crib to a larger area on the floor with a safety gate. She wants more freedom, and we provide a safe place for that freedom. She is growing, boundaries are changing, her trust in us is still growing. Now at age three, she is walking and talking and her safe space is the whole house. Her safe space is now partly within her; she has learned not to put small items in her mouth, not to run out the door into the street, and not to play with knives. She has trusted us to teach her boundaries, and we are trusting her to stay within the boundaries we have taught her. Mutual trust is now growing.

One of your goals as a mother is to wisely expand the "safe space" fence for your child. As she grows, the fence will need to grow, too, and you are going to play a major role in determining how much space she needs in that fence, how much of the fence is internalized within her, and how much still needs to be rigid and controlled by you. We want *mutual trust* to keep growing. We are not only helping to create the fence; we are a big part of the fence. Does she rely on us? Can she trust us with her feelings? Can she tell us her mistakes? Can we trust her? Can she handle more adult responsibility? This is how healthy boundaries and trust are established.

Boundaries need to be secure. Our kids always need to know there is some kind of fence. Even as an adult, I am blessed to have parents who still provide a fence, meaning—I know that if something tragic happens in my life, they will be there in whatever way they can. Even when I have difficulties in my relationship with my parents, I have a deep trust that they always want good for me. Secure boundaries will help teach your children to trust.

However, boundaries need to be flexible too. It often takes the pushing of limits to understand where the limits are supposed to be. I like to use that same picture of a fence and imagine it being made of a rubber band material. Our kids will often push hard on our fences to see how strong they are. My mom rules have changed throughout the years as I have changed, as our family has changed, and as each child has brought new challenges. I have to be willing to change the fence if it is not working anymore. I need to accept that "fence testing" is part of the growing up process and, at times, trust will be misplaced and broken. When that happens, we pick up and start building again.

9. Reject Comparison

Nothing good comes from comparison because it always leads to pride or envy. First, don't compare yourself to other moms. We are all intimately aware of our faults and failures and generally unaware of the faults and failures of others. That does not lead to a lot of happiness or gratitude in our own hearts. If you are a person who tends to perceive other people's faults much more than your own, you will not be able to hide your judgmental attitude. You cannot build heart-connected relationships with others when you have a judgmental spirit. Eventually the measure you use to judge others will be measured back to you (Matthew 7:1).

Something we do infrequently in homeschooling is standardized testing. Typically, I have my kids do state testing, beginning in fourth grade. Because I think my kids are great, I am often surprised that the standardized testing does not reflect their genius abilities (LOL). From an early age, I knew JD had a unique brain and a unique way of processing information. He blew through a lot of the childhood theories I had already developed with RW and Lissy. He was an early talker, a strange crawler, and could drop kick a ball at 18 months. I have never doubted his intelligence, but that did not stop my discouragement after he got his first set of standardized test scores. His scores did not seem to reflect the intelligence I was seeing. However, the Holy Spirit had led me earlier in the day to reflect on this verse from 2 Corinthians 10:12b, *But when they measure themselves by one another and compare themselves with one another, they are without understanding.* I was truly amazed! This verse opened my eyes to the fact that our entire system of measuring success in our children is based on comparison. This is without understanding. JD has his own God-given unique intelligence, and I do not need to evaluate it in comparison with his peers.

So, strive to get comparison out of your mind and heart because it is another relationship killer. Don't compare yourself with other women, don't compare your kids to other people's kids, and don't compare your own kids to each other (which I know is hard to do). Keep your eyes fixed on what God's Word, the Bible, says about all of us- we are all made in the image of God, and that is the truth.

10. Reject the Culture's Changing Standards

If you are going to be a mom who relentlessly pursues relationship with your kids, rather than performance and standards, then your life is going to look different. You cannot live up to the current culture's standards of parenting and be serious about building heart-connected relationships at the same time. You are going to eventually face a crisis of your convictions. It is bound to happen, so get ready for it.

You will have to make decisions that may not be popular with your friends or with your kids. For me, there was not just one, but several decisions, some big and some small. These decisions usually revolved around education, activities, friendships, and church.

While the culture around us can give us a message that we can "have it all," I have come to accept that is not true. I cannot do it all, have it all, or please the many voices that are giving me advice on the best way to raise children. I have to choose over and over again what are the most important things for me and my family. For example, RW, JD and Ray have all been on athletic teams that have games on Sundays. Being married to a pastor, Sundays are not only important days for family rest and enjoyment, they are also the day of the week that is set aside for church and worship. Pastor families have complicated Sundays because we desire to worship God as a family in church, but my husband also has several work responsibilities. The idea of taking kids to play in sporting events on Sunday does not support our family's belief that Sundays should be special from other days of the week. Additionally, it is logistically impossible to have so many people going in different directions. It is essential that our Sundays, our Sabbath days, are for God first, then families, and never sports first. Even compared to when RW was younger, there seems even more pressure to have kids play on travel teams with Sunday commitments. So while we do not have a hard and fast rule that our boys never can play sports on Sunday, we generally say, "No" to these kinds of sport commitments even if there are some negative consequences. The truth is, there typically are negative consequences, but at the same time it is amazing how God will open doors and honor your family in ways you may not expect because you are making choices to honor Him. *Living according to your convictions typically costs you something. If it never costs you anything, then maybe your convictions are not that valuable.*

My husband and I have decided that our relationships with God and with each other are going to be the most important things for us. When my kids grow up and start their own families, they will get to choose their most important things. We will encourage them to choose, and not just settle for the standards that culture places before them. Moms, we have the power to choose what will guide the decisions for our family, and we do not have to accept the status quo.

Your Relational Action Plan

So those are my top ten relational action plan points, but this is by no means a complete list. I certainly hope that you will soon be adding to this list as you pray and grow in your relationship with God and with your children. You have a lifetime with your kids to build heart-connected relationships.

Let me add one more important building block for good relationships: prayer. Sometimes our relationships can be so marred by hurt that we feel paralyzed. In these situations, action plans only make us feel more helpless. Praying for our kids and with our kids is always the best relational action plan. Remember that God is always working, even when we cannot see it and even when we cannot do any of the work ourselves. I would encourage you to always be in prayer, not only for your kids' problems, health, and successes, but also for your relationship with them. I once heard a pastor say that he prayed every day that he would be the "keeper of his children's hearts." I liked that idea. While I cannot say that I pray that each day, I do pray frequently that my children will give me their hearts. Rob and I love them and desire good for them all the days of their lives, so when they willingly give us their hearts, they are willing to listen to what we have to say. While we may not always agree with each other as time goes on, we do want to have great relationships with them that will last a lifetime.

Mom Mission #10

Build good relationships with your kids because
good relationships do not just happen.

Chapter 11
Wooers of Our Children's Hearts

What does it mean to woo a heart? While the phrase may seem old-fashioned, I find the concept of "wooing" very helpful as a Mom. Wooing is a word that is often used to describe the process of a man pursuing a woman: a process of kindness, attention and love notes to win the heart of someone in a romantic pursuit. It may seem strange to talk about "wooing" the hearts of our children, but I hope to show you in this chapter that the world is also wooing your children as well. What I mean is that we see examples of "wooing" all around us. Advertisers are trying to woo your heart so that you will fall in love with what they are trying to sell you. Politicians are wooing constituents to get their votes. You and your children are being "wooed" every day to give your heart, your loyalty, your passion, your resources, to one cause or another. So let me explain why *WE* should woo our children's hearts.

From the day a child is conceived (not born), a spiritual battle begins for the heart of the child. Growing up in church, I remember hearing repeatedly that God had a good plan for my life. But this is something I did *not* hear—Satan has a plan for my life, too. Look at John 10:10, *The thief comes only to steal and kill and destroy. I have come that they may have life, and have it to the full* (NIV). We naturally like to believe there is a good, powerful God we can turn to, but it is harder to accept that we have a powerful, evil, enemy working against us as well. Sometimes the enemy wins some battles in this life. We do not like to say this out loud, but let's be honest. I believe in eternity and I believe God will make all things right. This is one of the biggest lessons we learn from the death and resurrection of Jesus Christ. Ultimately, Satan does not win the war, but he does win battles here in this life. Children are, and always have been, the most vulnerable people group in this world because they can be controlled and abused by adults who do not value them. Children need loving protectors.

Loving and protecting is part of God's plan—not Satan's plan. As the weakest and most vulnerable part of our society, children are most often victimized. It is incredibly powerful that one of the first mission works of the early Christians in Rome was to save the babies who had been abandoned to die on the rocks outside the city. In ancient Rome, the father had the power to decide whether he wanted to keep his baby or abandon it. Keep in mind that ancient Rome was the most advanced of all ancient civilizations. Yet even here, the value of children was completely dependent on the decision of the father. The custom was that eight-day-old babies would be placed at the feet of the father and after inspection, he could determine whether he would accept or reject the baby. The rejected babies were abandoned at the rocks.

It was the early Christians who understood that God valued *all human life* regardless of color, sex, status, or *age*. Jesus taught them specifically that God valued children! God esteemed children. It is hard to understand just how countercultural this was in the ancient world. It was the early Christians who daily went to the rocks to save those babies. God loves life, and Satan loves death.

I am sure you are wondering why I am dragging you into an ancient history lesson, so here is my point. A spiritual battle for the heart of children is nothing new. It is not just a battle for physical life but for spiritual life, too. Proverbs 4:23 is one of my favorite verses: *Guard your heart above all else, for it determines the course of your life* (NLT). Why is there a spiritual battle raging for the heart of your child? It is because the heart of your child will determine the course of your child's life.

Mom, you are in a battle to be the keeper of your child's heart. You are to be the first guardian of your children's hearts because you love them and you desire what is best for them. Does the world love your children? No. The world wants to influence your children. Satan wants to destroy your children. God desires for parents to love and bless their children as well as help them reach their greatest potential. He also wants them to have life to the fullest as they come to know and follow Him.

I have done my best to explain the battle. Now I want to tell you how to win it!

You Cannot Demand Consideration

I am a sensitive person, and I am a people person. I have some sensitive and people-pleasing kids. For those of you who understand this personality, you know that a lot of the drama in your home can revolve around relationships and hurt feelings. So, I have dried many tears (my own and my children's) regarding rejection from friendships, extended family members, siblings, and so on and so forth. Rejection is a painful and powerful emotion that has a domino effect on a lot of other negative emotions such as depression, jealousy, and anger. Feelings of rejection in ourselves and our kids need to be dealt with directly.

One day a friend said to me in a passing conversation, "Amy, you cannot demand consideration." This was a teachable moment. I cannot demand that people treat me the way I want to be treated. I cannot demand to be included. I cannot demand to be accepted. I cannot demand people pay attention to me or my feelings. I cannot demand people's favor or approval. Simply, I cannot demand their love or their affection. Hearts do not work that way.

I found myself saying that to my kids quite frequently. When my daughter Milly was experiencing the loss of a friendship or on the lonely end of mean comments, I would use this as an opportunity to teach her that she cannot demand consideration. While we can pray for people who hurt us, and may sometimes need to confront people who hurt us (Matthew 18:15), we cannot demand someone's consideration. We cannot demand that someone like us. We cannot demand their heart.

Do you realize this is true of all human relationships? You cannot demand consideration from anyone. I realize that there can be a lot of fake consideration. An employer can require you to treat people well, but that does not mean you actually care about them. A teacher can require students to be kind to each other in the classroom, but that does not mean there is genuine friendship. You cannot demand a person give you their heart—you have to woo a heart, even the hearts of your children.

How Do You Woo a Heart?

Again, read Romans 2:4 (NLT). *Don't you see how wonderfully kind, tolerant, and patient God is with you? Can't you see that his kindness is intended to turn you from your sin?*

God surrounds His people with lovingkindness. While God desires us to obey Him, serve Him, and worship Him—let us not forget that it His lovingkindness that draws our hearts to Him. If the God of the universe, who is perfect and worthy of all praise, does not demand the hearts of His people but instead He woos the hearts of His people through His kindness, why do we think we can demand the hearts of our own children?

As a Mom, you do have the right to demand certain things from your children. We can demand respect and respect can be given. We can demand obedience and we can get obedience. We can demand lots of different behaviors, standards, and rules that need to be followed in our homes. But we can never demand our children's hearts. We cannot demand their consideration, affection, devotion, or love. Our children's hearts will need to be wooed and won, just as God woos and wins our hearts through His lovingkindness.

Psalm 117:2 is a beautiful verse to meditate on, write down, and have displayed in your home. *For His lovingkindness prevails over us [and we triumph and overcome through Him], And the truth of the LORD endures forever. Praise the LORD! (Hallelujah!)* (AMP).

God's lovingkindness is the truth that endures forever. You can woo your kids' hearts through the power of your lovingkindness towards them.

Love Will Win the Battle for Our Children's Hearts

I have a dear friend who went through an ugly divorce. There was a lot of animosity and hostility from her soon-to-be ex-husband. Because he had a lot of money and other resources, it often felt that the cards were stacked against her. She had to submit many of her parenting decisions to the courts. Many things were out of her control. When her kids would spend every other weekend away from her, they were exposed to situations and things that would make her cringe.

There was a lot of prayer, a lot of tears, and there was something that I continually reminded her of: the battle for her kids was not happening in the courts but in the hearts of her children. Her sacrificial life demonstrated to her kids that she loved them with selfless love. Many times it seemed like she was losing the battle, whether it was decisions from the courts or the lure of a father who could give them anything they wanted. However, she never gave up. Her daily sacrificial love showed the children how much their mother cared about their lives. While their father tried to demand their hearts, or buy their affection, she persistently demonstrated lovingkindness. This did not mean she did not discipline them; it meant that she never gave up on them. She wooed them with the lovingkindness that she was receiving from her heavenly Father. While she may have lost some battles in the courts, over time she won the battle for her children's hearts.

Moms, you can do this! You can woo your kids' hearts through lovingkindness. All of those steps in the relational action plan can be rooted in lovingkindness. I know when we look at this scary world we can see all the battles ahead of our kids. We can see how the culture around us wants to have the hearts of our kids, which brings them all sorts of trouble. It is not possible to keep our kids from ALL trouble. They will make mistakes—big ones! They will fail and fail again. They will experience rejection and pain that we cannot rescue them from. They will have problems, big and small. But we can be there for them. We can have great influence not only when they are little, but throughout their lives, because we have consistently pursued heart-connected relationships with them. We have loved them for who they are *and* who they are becoming, and they know it. That is true success for all of us not-so-perfect moms.

Mom Mission #11

Woo and win the hearts of your children.

Chapter 12
Become a Pioneer

Throw open the doors
You know my heart is yours
What are we waitin' for?
Let's be Pioneers
And we'll build a home
In the great unknown
Yeah, let's be pioneers.
–for King and Country

For some time now, I have tried to adopt a pioneer philosophy. Maybe it is just my obsession with Laura Ingalls Wilder, but I have found a resonance with viewing my life from a pioneer perspective. The group King and Country has a song titled "Let's Be Pioneers," and when I heard it, I felt like they had been reading my mind for the past ten years. "Building a home in the great unknown" is a phrase that resonates with a message that God used in my life over the past several years to encourage me.

While I enjoyed the *Little House on the Prairie* television show as a girl growing up in the 1970s, it was through my homeschooling journey that I began reading the books to my children. When we started studying the history of the pioneers, I made a connection that I had not made before. I realized that while the pioneers were living simply on the frontier, the people back on the East Coast were living with all the modern conveniences.

For example, did you know the Biltmore house in Asheville, North Carolina was built between 1889 and 1895? Although I have never been there myself, my friends and family have described the opulence. The Biltmore is still the largest privately-owned house in the United States. This was the same time that Laura Ingalls Wilder and her family were living primitively in a log cabin in the Midwest. I had not considered that American pioneers chose to leave more modern homes and conveniences for a much harsher lifestyle, because they had the vision for a much different—and better—way of life. So many pioneers left the modern comforts of their day, their extended families, and comfortable homes in exchange for a life of hardship in the great unknown.

It took a large amount of courage, firm resolution, and vision for a different life to survive as a pioneer. I can only imagine the pressure they must have received to forego such a dangerous new life. I think many extended families were quite upset with their relatives' decision to leave, knowing they could be saying "good-bye" forever. Do you think you could have maintained your vision for a better life in the midst of hardships, dangers, and incredible personal sacrifice? In our current society, despite sending our brave military families and missionaries to faraway places, I do not think we can even comprehend such level of sacrifice.

I do not really compare my life to the brave pioneers, but this is how I began to personally connect with their stories. I did not grow up in a large family. I did not grow up in ministry life. (My dad was a successful businessman.) I did not grow up being homeschooled. But one day, the Lord impressed on my heart that Rob and I were pioneering a new way of raising our family. The choices we were making would eventually mean we had to leave things behind. Okay, we did not move to Africa or overseas, so I am not trying to lay claim that we have made major sacrifices in that way. I also cannot claim a life of true hardship, but I am saying that I had to learn to make sacrifices.

By viewing myself through this pioneer perspective, it gave me courage to forge a new way of life for our family. I could more easily accept some of the sacrifices that we were making. Having seven kids meant we could not do some of the things that other families could do in regard to activities or vacations. At one point, I saw that as a sacrifice I needed to accept...but because of this pioneer vision, I have been able to hold on to the fact that we are *choosing* to do life differently. We had a vision for a different—and hopefully better—life for our kids and future grandchildren. Eagerly, I accepted the new adventures that God was laying in our path without fear. And God's journey for our family has led us to unexpected places. Through Visionary Family Ministries, we have been able to participate in family mission trips to France, Moldova, Ukraine, Scotland, Moscow, and the Dominican Republic. I never dreamed that our family would have these kinds of opportunities!

When you embrace your mission to develop real, heart-connected relationships with your kids, you are choosing a different path, a pioneer path. Your life will look dissimilar from many of your friends. There will be sacrifices. We cannot have it all. The sacrifices might be giving up a satisfying career path in order to have more time for your family. Or it may be working an extra job because you need to make money to help your kids have an opportunity at a good school. As a single mom, it might be prioritizing your relationships with your kids above an opportunity to start a new relationship. Sacrifices come in all shapes and sizes. Do not try to compare the sacrifices you make with anyone else's. God put me through many tests of little sacrifices and then much bigger ones. At times, the little ones were even harder. It is often difficult to yield the small luxuries in life that we feel we are entitled to have.

When I was first married, I had time to decorate my house—but no money to do it. Then after having lots of little children, I had no time, money, or energy to decorate my house to my liking. When I started homeschooling, just keeping my house basically clean and organized was my daily battle. Decorating was a pipe dream! When I went to other women's homes that looked beautiful, I would easily become jealous and then discontented with my own surroundings. But then the Lord gently led me to a pioneer perspective. I was *choosing* this life. Some of my disgruntled attitude about my home could have been fixed if I had chosen to get a part-time job and put my kids in school. However, I liked the fruit that God was bringing out of this life my husband and I were creating in our "great unknown." I liked the fruit so much, that it was well worth the sacrifice. I became much more content that my life did not look like other moms I knew. None of us have the exact same lives.

It is unwise to compare our situation with other moms we know. We have to keep our focus on the vision God has given us for our own life. Our pioneer plot was just for us. I realized we were all happy with this life, so why should I complain?

God will lead you on your own pioneer path if you will let Him. There are a lot of ways we can choose a different path. While it will involve sacrifice, it is often in leaving behind some things that we find more freedom and more open space in our lives for relationships and love.

Do you have a pioneer vision for your role as a mom? It is amazing how much happiness you will discover when you start following God's path for **you**. The pioneer path is challenging and not for the faint of heart, but it is also rewarding. You can have life-long influence on the hearts of your children and grandchildren. These children will love you back with affection and gratitude. This is a wonderful reward! Your influence will also have a ripple effect on our culture, which is another reward. What does our culture need? Godly children—children who know how to love well. Remember how special you are, Mom. You are an important part of God's plan for making this happen. We can see change in our world through the love of not-so-perfect moms.

Mom Mission #12

Choose your own pioneer path.

Conclusion

Happiness. If you remember, we started this journey talking about happiness. As moms, we want happy children. Not children who need to have everything perfect in order to be happy, but children who are happy in the ups and downs of life because they know they are loved for who they are, not for what they do or how well they measure up to the changing standards of success that are set before them. True happiness does not come from our circumstances. Happiness comes from being loved. I am convinced that learning to love well is one of the main reasons that God gives us children. How else would we learn that love comes from self-sacrifice and not self-indulgence?

However, this book has not been primarily about raising happy children, but instead about becoming happy moms. God wants you to be happy because He loves you and you are His child. This world needs happy moms. Psalm 144:15b reads, *The people whose God is the LORD are truly happy!* (CEB). Now I understand that many translations of the Bible use the word *blessed* instead of *happy.* And here at the end of this book, I am not going to dive into a word study to discuss the nuances of different Biblical translations. Blessed is a good word as well. We are blessed to be loved by God, we are blessed to have children, we are blessed as Christians to be free of our sins and mistakes. All of this is true. But let me tell you why I like the word happy instead of blessed. It is because I can *SEE HAPPY.* True happiness is visible. I like to *see* happy moms. Kids like to *see* happy moms.

Because I have been privileged to travel around the country and the world serving and talking with moms, I have had firsthand experience seeing moms who have been worn thin, weary, anxious, and guilt-ridden. Moms who carry the unconscious drive of perfectionism which daily robs them of happiness. Even as I write this book, I can still find myself falling into this same trap, which leads to negative thinking and an unhappy face. It is a daily choice, a minute-by-minute choice, to put my hope in a perfect God who does have a perfect plan that I can trust, even in the midst of all the imperfect. I understand that just as I like to see my children happy, God likes to see me happy. When I can still smile and enjoy life, even in the midst of all the problems and difficulties, God is blessed. God is blessed when His children trust Him. God is happy when I trust Him. God is happy when you trust Him.

I hope as you finish this book, you are a little happier! I hope you feel a little lighter and a little more free. The world needs happy moms, but more importantly, your kids will like a happy YOU! May you rest in the fact that God is working in your life. I hope that your vision for who YOU are as a mom got bigger and more attainable at the same time. You are free to be the best not-so-perfect mom that God created you to be.

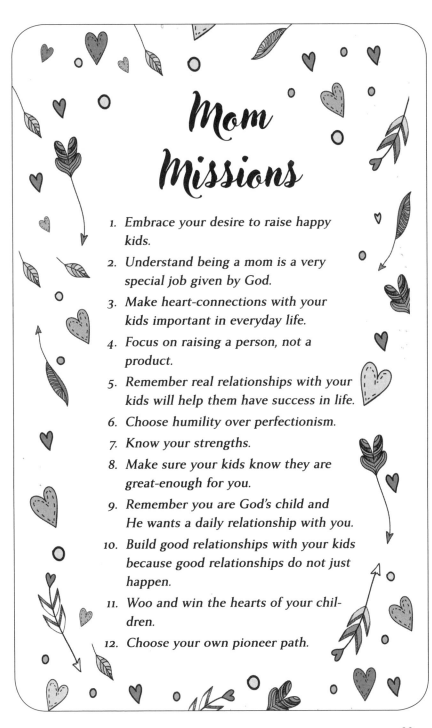

Mom Missions

1. *Embrace your desire to raise happy kids.*
2. *Understand being a mom is a very special job given by God.*
3. *Make heart-connections with your kids important in everyday life.*
4. *Focus on raising a person, not a product.*
5. *Remember real relationships with your kids will help them have success in life.*
6. *Choose humility over perfectionism.*
7. *Know your strengths.*
8. *Make sure your kids know they are great-enough for you.*
9. *Remember you are God's child and He wants a daily relationship with you.*
10. *Build good relationships with your kids because good relationships do not just happen.*
11. *Woo and win the hearts of your children.*
12. *Choose your own pioneer path.*

Notes

[1] The original quote is, "If a thing is worth doing, it is worth doing badly." "Chapter 14." *What's Wrong with the World*, by G. K. Chesterton, Limovia. net, 2014.

[2] "Training Children in Godliness." *Training Children in Godliness*, by Jacob Abbott and Michael J. McHugh, Christian Liberty Press, 1992, p. 117.

[3] https://biblehub.com/commentaries/pulpit/exodus/2.htm.

[4] https://www.bibletimelines.com/timelines/moses--the-exodus-timeline.

[5] *The Hand that Rocks the Cradle*. www.potw.org/archive/potw391.html.

[6] Mother Teresa. *A Simple Path*. Ballantine Books, 1995.

[7] "Bowlby Attachment Theory - Core *Emotional Development in Humans*." *Explorable - Think Outside The Box - Research, Experiments, Psychology, Self-Help*, explorable.com/bowlby-attachment-theory.

[8] "Maternal Deprivation." *John Bowlby and Attachment Theory*, by Jeremy Holmes, Routledge, 2014.

[9] Macaulay, Susan Schaeffer. *For the Children's Sake: Foundations of Education for Home and School*. Crossway Books, 2009, p 12-13.

[10] Fielding, Jonathan. "Loneliness Is an Emerging Public Health Threat." *The Hill*, The Hill, 9 Oct. 2018, thehill.com/opinion/healthcare/410500-loneliness-is-an-emerging-public-health-threat.

[11] "Sink Reflections." *Sink Reflections*, by Marla Cilley, Bantam Books, 2004, p. 14.

[12] "What Is a 'Good Enough Mother'?" *Psychology Today*, Sussex Publishers, www.psychologytoday.com/us/blog/suffer-the-children/201605/what-is-good-enough-mother.

[13] "Webster's Dictionary 1828 - Affection." *Websters Dictionary 1828*, webstersdictionary1828.com/Dictionary/affection.

VISIONARY FAMILY
MINISTRIES

Rob and Amy Rienow founded Visionary Family Ministries in 2011 to encourage and equip families to live for Christ and pass faith through the generations.

Find encouragement for your family, and learn more about hosting a Visionary Family Conference in your community at www.VisionaryFam.com

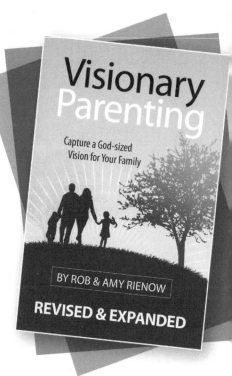

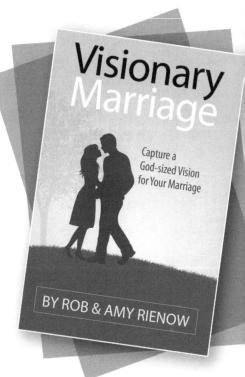

What is **D6**?

BASED ON DEUTERONOMY 6:4-7

A **conference** for your entire **team**

A **curriculum** for every age at **church**

An **experience** for every person in your **home**

Connecting
CHURCH & HOME
These must work together!

D6 CONFERENCE
ONCE A YEAR

DEFINE & REFINE Your Discipleship Plan

ONE HOUR
A WEEK

www.d6family.com

POWER OF
PARENTAL INFLUENCE